COMPACT
CYMRU

CW00516933

The Tic

David George Bowers

Gwasg Carreg Gwalch

First published in 2021
© text: David George Bowers

ISBN: 978-1-84524-314-2
Cover design: Eleri Owen

Published by Gwasg Carreg Gwalch,
12 Iard yr Orsaf, Llanrwst, Wales LL26 0EH
tel: 01492 642031
email: books@carreg-gwalch.cymru
website: www.carreg-gwalch.cymru

Acknowledgements

Any book is a team effort. This one would
not have been possible without the
enthusiasm and help of Myrddin ap Dafydd
and the staff of the publisher, Gwasg Carreg
Gwalch, especially Mererid Jones for
preparing this book under exceptional
circumstances. I am grateful to Steve
Groom, Peter Miller and Dan Clewley at
NEODAAS in Plymouth for help with the
satellite pictures and for giving permission
to use them. Satellite data used in chapter
2 were received and processed by the UK's
NERC Earth Observation Data Acquisition
and Analysis Service (NEODAAS) at
Dundee University and Plymouth Marine
Laboratory (http://www.neodaas.ac.uk).
SeaWiFS data were provided courtesy of
the NASA SeaWiFS project and Orbital
Sciences Corporation. The spectacular
kayaking photos in chapter 3 were kindly
provided by the Preseli Venture Adventure
Centre in North Pembrokeshire. I have
enjoyed discussions about topics in this
book with Rick Nunes-Vaz, Alan Elliott,
John Simpson, Martyn Roberts, Alan
Davies, Toby Sherwin, Suzie Jackson, Tim
Whitton and many others, sometimes in
the cosy snug of the Liverpool Arms in
Menai Bridge. David Roberts of the School
of Ocean Sciences at Bangor University
took the superb aerial photographs. The
staff of the National Library of Wales in
Aberystwyth were very helpful about
providing historic documents and charts. I
would also like to thank the staff at
Fishguard Public Library for their help. My
thanks go to Chris Knibbs for the details of
the flooding of the car park in Fishguard.
Finally, my long-suffering wife, Faith, not
only put up with me writing another book
but accompanied me on some of the trips
for this one. That made touring the
beautiful Welsh coastline even more
enjoyable.

Contents

Image page 1: Whitesands Bay, St David's
Above: Dunes by the Mawddach

The word tide *comes from the Old English 'tid' meaning time.*

The Welsh word for tide is llanw, *commonly used with an adjective, as in* penllanw *for high tide and* llanw isel *for low tide.*

1. Raising Tides

It is unusual to see a book about the tides of a single country. Tides fill the global ocean and the laws that govern them are universal. A book about tides in Wales is akin to, for example, one about rainbows in Madagascar. So, what's so special about Welsh tides to make them merit this book?

Along its relatively short coastline, Wales manages to pack in some of the greatest tidal phenomena on our planet. On a journey around the Welsh coast you can see the largest rise and fall of the tide in Europe (and in the world, outside Canada). Tidal currents rush through channels and around headlands at speeds faster than the Gulf Stream. Undulating tidal bores power their way into the nation's rivers, there are hydraulic jumps loved by adventurous kayakers, tidal whirlpools and the rarest of tidal phenomena, double high waters. Tides mix seawater, dispersing pollutants, pushing salt up estuaries and storing the summer heat of the sun to make our characteristic mild (but wet) Welsh winters. It is a fact that many of the subtleties of tidal mixing were first discovered in Welsh coastal and offshore waters and then found to be important wherever there are tides. Historically, Welsh people have always been exceptionally good at using the tide. They made traps to catch fish and tide mills to grind wheat (the tide provided the country with its loaves *and* its fishes). As we move to an uncertain energy future, the great Welsh tides can be harnessed as a clean and reliable source of energy.

Wales is a great showcase for tides and what they can do. Welsh tides deserve a book of their own.

The tide at the beach

Let's begin at the place most people first encounter the tide: at the beach. Beaches change their size and their appearance with the state of the tide. Arrive at a large beach when the sea is low and the tide is out and you will see an expanse of mud,

1. Low tide at a beach is a good time to explore rock pools and for beach-combers to find what the sea has left behind; 2. High tide washes away the footprints and allows storm breakers to run up to the shore.

5

The Tides of Wales

rock and sand. This is a good time for families to look for marine life in rock pools and for dogs to use up their energy. On days after a new or full moon, when the sea retreats furthest, fishers have their best chance of digging for bait-worms and archaeologists and treasure-hunters can explore sands that are exposed just a few times each year. As the sea rises, the beach users have to be careful not to be cut off from the safety of the shore. The tide advances at a moderate pace up most Welsh beaches (slower than walking pace), but there is a danger that channels will fill the space between you and safety. The incoming sea smoothes the sand and rubs out footprints, re-creating a pristine beach ready for the next day. At high tide, the beach can shrink to a narrow strand of sand and pebbles battered in winter by

3. Lines of seaweed left by successive tides on Aberystwyth beach; 4. Driftwood deposited by storm waves and high tides on the shingle beach at Barry; 5. Bands on a cliff made by different coloured algae tolerant to different tide levels; 6. A lake on Penmon beach that fills and empties as the tide percolates through the pebbles.

storm waves that, on a Welsh beach, can have travelled thousands of miles from an Atlantic storm. At the top of the beach you will see lines of detritus, broken bits of seaweed and other flotsam deposited by the tide. This is a visible memory of how high the tide can reach, each successive line being created by a different tide. Large pieces of driftwood are sometimes left on the beach and, when dried out, these can provide a useful source of timber. There is a cottage on Anglesey with ceiling beams made with hardwood left by wrecks of the Spanish Armada. I'm told that driftwood carried up the river Wye to Tintern in Gwent is still collected and chopped up to be sold as firewood. A more permanent visual memory of tide levels are the bands of colour on a cliff or rock. The bands are a vertical slice through the *intertidal zone*: a place which is covered by water when the tide is in and uncovered when the tide is out. The coloured bands are made by different species of algae and lichen that can tolerate different levels of exposure to the air or immersion in the sea. They find (or have to fight for) the level on the rock that is best for them.

From the beach you may see a tidal island which you can walk to at low water but which is cut off at high water. There are dozens of tidal islands in Wales, some more accessible than others (tidal islands are popular in fiction, including novels by Agatha Christie and Robert Louis Stevenson). There are also tidal lakes, depressions in the beach that fill and empty with the tide. One at Penmon on Anglesey was just a dry hollow when we arrived at the beach; two hours later it was half-filled with salt water that had percolated through the mound of pebbles between it and the sea.

The rhythm of the tide

Tides around the world have the same set of rhythms, produced by the motion of the earth, moon and sun. The tides of the Welsh coast, like those of most of the world, are half daily, or *semi-diurnal*. There are two high tides and two low tides each day. The high waters succeed each other at a mean interval of 12 hours and 25 minutes. Each full day, the time of high tide advances by twice 25 minutes, or 50 minutes on average. If high tide today is at 2pm, expect high tide tomorrow at about 2.50pm and so on. Graphs showing the variation of water depth with time are called a *tidal curve* and contain all the information about how sea level varies at a place including any departures from a smooth, regular and symmetrical curve. Alternatively, the principal facts about the tide on a single day or a series of days at a place can be presented as a table of the times and heights of high and low waters, for example:

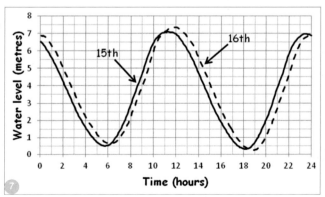

7. *The rise and fall of the tide at Menai Bridge on two consecutive days.*

	Time	Height (m)
Low tide	05:45	0.50
High tide	11:12	7.09
Low tide	18:16	0.32
High tide	23:29	6.98

Daily times and heights for high and low tides at important places around the coast are easily found in newspapers and on the internet. Monthly tables are posted by the council at ports and popular beaches and books of yearly tide tables are available in shops. Tide poles, often placed at the

8. *Bilingual tide tables on Aberystwyth promenade; 9. A tide pole outside Conwy marina. The zero level on the pole (Lowest Astronomical Tide or LAT) is the lowest level that the tide would normally fall to at that place.*

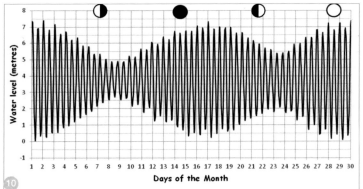

10. *The variation of water level at Menai Bridge over a month, with the phases of the moon.*

datum. The figures on the chart then give the minimum depth of water, to which the height of the tide can be added to give the actual depth at any time.

The vertical rise of sea level between low tide and high tide is called the *tidal range* and this varies during the month with the phase of the moon. The largest tidal range in the semi-diurnal tide occurs shortly after the times of new and full moon; these are called spring tides (to do with a springing up of water rather than the season of the year). At spring tides, the high waters reach their highest level and, in addition, the low waters sink to their lowest level. Spring tides happen twice a month, at an interval of 15 days and (in Wales) can be reckoned to occur one or two days after a new or full moon. Half way between spring tides (and so one or two days after the quarter moon) lies a period of minimum tidal range, called a neap tide.

The half-daily semi-diurnal and 15-day springs-neaps cycles are the main rhythms

entrance to a harbour, show the height of the tide. The height on these poles (and on the tide tables) is measured from a fixed level called a *datum*. A commonly used datum in the UK and many other countries is the lowest level to which the tide would normally be expected to fall at a place: a level called the *Lowest Astronomical Tide* (or LAT). Under extreme weather conditions, the sea may fall below LAT but this would be exceptional. Depths on Admiralty charts are also measured relative to LAT and so this level of lowest tide is also called *chart* to the tide but there are others. Over the course of a full year, the high waters are highest (and the low waters lowest) at the equinoxes in March and September. There are smaller tidal ranges in mid-summer and mid-winter. Each month, one of the spring tides is usually higher than the other. This happens because the moon's orbit about the earth is elliptical. The earth-moon distance varies over the month and on one of the spring tides the moon is closer, making bigger tides.

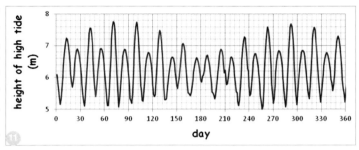

The tide needs to be taken into account when drawing maps of the coastline and when measuring heights relative to sea level. The long-term average sea level (mean sea level) is the datum used for measuring the heights of mountains on Ordnance Survey maps and is called Ordnance Datum. There is therefore a difference between ordnance datum and chart datum which will depend on the local tidal range. Chart datum will be lower than Ordnance datum by a distance equal to half the maximum tidal range at that place. Another concept used on Ordnance Survey maps is the level of high and low water on

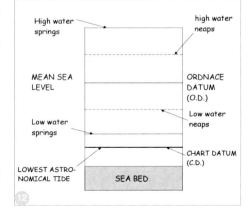

11. *Heights (above LAT) of the high tides at Milford Haven over the course of a year;*
12. *Tide levels.*

High Tide Route
Llwybr Llanw Uchel

Low Tide Route
Llwybr Llanw Isel

Llwybr Arfordir Cymru
Wales Coast Path

MAE
CLOGWYNI'N
LLADD
CADWCH
AT Y
LLWYBR

13. *Tidal alternatives on the coast path.*

an *ordinary tide*; these are used to mark the positions of the shoreline at high and low water. An ordinary tide lies midway between neaps and springs.

It has to be acknowledged that even the fastest tidal rhythms are slow by impatient human standards. Occasionally the tide rouses itself to do something dramatic, creating turbulent water or a river bore, but generally speaking watching and waiting for the tide slows the pace of your life. This can be very pleasant. A good way to get into the tidal rhythm, for example, is to take a walk along part of the Welsh coast path, which runs along the whole coastline mostly close to the sea. During a day's walk on this national trail you can see the tide coming in and going out again and get familiar with its rhythms. Sometimes, the course of the path itself changes to take account of the tide.

Tidal streams

For those who travel on – or under – the sea, the horizontal movement of water associated with the tide can be just as important, or more so, than the rise and fall of the sea surface. The currents, or tidal *streams*, around Wales can be fast. A boat can be slowed down by an adverse stream or, conversely, speeded up by a favourable one. In many places, it would be hopeless for a swimmer to try to make headway against the tide; the flow is just too strong.

For those of us watching from the shore, it is not so easy to see tidal currents. An exception is in an estuary or tidal river. When the tide is rising in the estuary, water flows in from the sea – upstream – and then turns and flows out again when the tide is falling. The name for the flow inland is the *flood* and the flow out is called the *ebb*. It is a common experience in the rather shallow estuaries that we have in Wales that the currents are faster on the flood and that the ebb flow lasts longer to compensate for this. A fast, short flood and longer, slower, ebb are the rule. When it's possible to measure the speed of the current at different depths, it is noticeable that the speed decreases towards the bottom, an effect of the friction of the estuary bed. As the flood turns to ebb, or vice versa, there is a short period of no current called *slack water*. Slack water in an estuary occurs at, or a little after, the time of high water and again at, or a little after, low water.

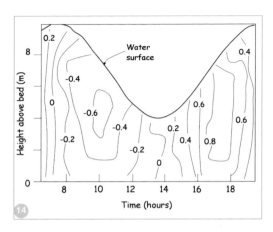

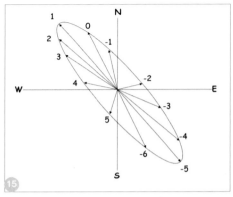

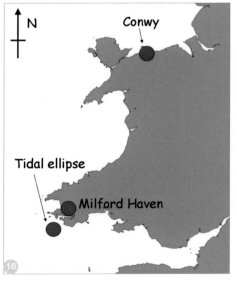

14. *Tidal currents in the Conwy estuary plotted against time and depth. Positive values are flood currents in metres per second;*
15. *Plot of surface currents over a tidal cycle based on observations on Admiralty Chart no. 2878. Figures refer to hours after high water at Milford Haven. The speed at hour 0 is 1.7 knots;*
16. *Map shows location of the Conwy and of the tidal diamond used in 15.*

The currents in an estuary are constrained to flow within the river's banks and so travel directly in or out, but in the open sea other directions are possible. In the coastal waters of Wales there is usually a predominant ebb and flood direction but between these the current can turn and flow in other directions. If the current is plotted each hour as an arrow showing speed and direction, the tip of the arrow traces out a curve which is approximately elliptical in shape. The current is fastest when the arrow points along the major axis of the ellipse and weakest when it points along the minor axis. Now there is no slack water, just a variation in the strength and direction of the current over the tidal cycle.

The origin of the tide

Tides are made by the gravitational pull of the moon (and, to a lesser extent, the sun) acting on the oceans. The earth and moon orbit, once a month, about their common centre of gravity (this is the key; we are used to the idea of the moon orbiting earth, but actually the earth and moon orbit each other about a point close to, but not exactly at, the earth's centre). The force that keeps them in this orbit, and stops them flying apart, is their mutual gravitational attraction. At the centre of the earth, the moon's gravity is exactly right to hold the earth in its orbit but, because the moon's gravity decreases with distance from the moon, it is stronger than it needs to be on the earth hemisphere closest to the moon and weaker than it needs to be in the hemisphere furthest

17. The principle of tide generation in an ocean covering the earth. The red arrows represent the moon's tidal forces on the earth.

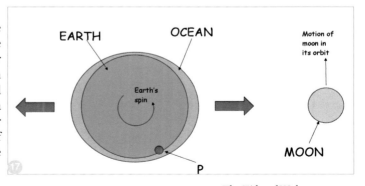

from the moon. This excess, or deficit, in the moon's gravity is the moon's *tidal force*. We can calculate this force at any point on the surface of the earth as the difference between the moon's gravity at that point and the moon's gravity at the centre of the earth. Tidal forces act towards the moon on the earth hemisphere facing the moon and away from the moon in the other earth hemisphere.

If the earth were covered in an ocean, the tidal forces would pull the water into two bulges: one directly beneath the moon and the other on the far side of the earth to the moon. As the earth spins on its axis, a point on the surface of the earth will experience two high tides a day as it passes through the bulges, with low tides between the bulges. In addition, in the 24 hours it

18. *Tides are made by a combination of the pull of the moon and sun. They are greatest when the moon and sun are in line with the earth, at times of new and full moon ...*
19. *... and smallest when the moon and sun make a right angle with the earth, at quarter moons.*

takes the earth to turn once on its axis, the moon moves some of the way around its orbit and the earth has to turn a little further to catch up with this motion of the moon. The time required to experience two high waters and two low waters is 24 hours and 50 minutes – a period of time called a *lunar day*. A lunar day can be divided into 24 lunar hours, so that a lunar hour is about one hour and two minutes of ordinary, solar, time.

The sun also exerts tidal forces on the earth. The sun is much more massive than the moon but it is also a lot further away; as a result the sun's tidal forces are smaller than those of the moon. At times of new and full moon, the earth, moon and sun are in line and the tidal forces combine to create spring tides. At the quarter moons, the moon and sun make a right angle with the earth and their forces tend to cancel, making weaker, neap tides. The rather complicated movement of the earth, moon and sun creates other rhythms in the tide. The moon's distance from earth varies over the month and the largest moon-created tides occur on the day of the month when the moon is closest to us. Semi-diurnal tides are greatest when the moon and sun lie in the plane of the equator. The largest tides of the year occur at the equinoxes – in March and September – when the sun is over the equator. Particularly large tides occur if the moon is also over the equator at the equinox. The largest tides of all occur when both moon and sun lie in the plane of the equator and both are at their closest distance to the earth. As time advances, the rhythms in the motion of the moon

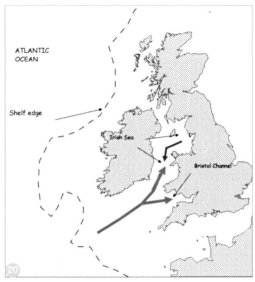

and sun move in and out of phase and the size of the tide responds to these changes.

The real oceans on our planet are bounded by continents and this stops the water flowing into tidal bulges (in fact,

20. *The tide travels as a wave from the edge of the continental shelf (red arrows) into the Irish Sea where it is reflected back off the coast near Liverpool (blue arrow). Part of the wave travels into the Bristol channel, but here the reflection is not so strong.*

even if the earth *were* covered in water, the bulges would not be able to travel fast enough to maintain their position under the moon as the earth turned). Instead, the variation of the tidal forces as the earth spins beneath the moon and sun creates waves in the ocean, in the same way that a paddle moving back and forth at the end of a long channel creates waves. In the case of the tide, the waves have the same period as the tidal forcing: the moon creates waves with a period of 12 hours and 25 minutes. In an ocean basin, such as the North Atlantic, the tidal wave travels around the ocean in such a way that the height of the wave is largest at the outer edge of the ocean and diminishes to nothing in the centre. You can create this type of wave by gently swirling a part-filled cup of tea. In the ocean these waves travel, for the most part, in an anti-clockwise direction in the northern hemisphere and clockwise in the southern, although there are exceptions to this rule. The important thing for us is that, at any point in the Atlantic, the level of the surface rises and falls every 12 lunar hours. Wales is not strictly on the North Atlantic but lies on what is called the *continental shelf* – an extension of the continent of Europe that was flooded as the glaciers melted at the end of the last ice age. The seas around Wales, and indeed the British Isles, are shallow – no more than 200 metres deep (compared to the average depth of the Atlantic of about 4000m). This shallowness extends for some hundreds of kilometres offshore to the shelf edge, where the sea bed plunges down to the ocean abyss. The rise and fall of the Atlantic at the shelf edge creates waves which travel across the continental shelf towards Wales. The waves cross the shelf south of Ireland and then divide at the south-west corner of Wales so that some of the wave travels up the Bristol Channel and the rest travels up the Irish Sea towards north Wales. When these incoming waves hit the coastline, they bounce off, or reflect.

The tide waves travelling across the continental shelf have the same period as the tide wave in the Atlantic Ocean, so the time interval between one high tide (or wave crest) and the next is 12 hours and 25 minutes. The waves travel quickly – the crest crosses the ground at a speed of about 100 kilometres per hour. The waves are also long: the distance between one crest and another is several hundred kilometres, so only a fraction of a wave fits on the continental shelf at any time. The slope of the surface in these waves is so gentle that a ship at sea is completely unaware of them as they travel across the shelf. When the wave crests followed by the bottom of the wave (or trough) reach the shore they create the rise and fall of the tide that we see at the coast.

The fact that these long tide waves are very good at reflecting off the coast allows the continental shelf to resonate with the tidal forcing at the shelf edge. The principle is exactly the same as that of an organ pipe: a small regular oscillation at the edge of the resonating system can produce large oscillations within it. As a result, the tide on the shelf is amplified compared to the ocean. The tidal range at the shelf break is small: generally only about 1 metre, but this can rise to 10 metres or more at the coast.

In principle, the known speed of the wave across the continental shelf could be used to prepare tide tables showing the times and heights of high and low water at a port. This would be equivalent to the way that weather forecasts are made. Starting

from known conditions, the likely future weather is forecast from the way that the atmosphere is likely to evolve. At the moment, however, tide tables are made in a different way, using the fact that the tide can be broken down mathematically into its various rhythms (called harmonics). Observations of the tide at a port are analysed to reveal the size and the timing of the tidal rhythms and, once that is done, the rhythms can then be projected into the future to predict tides accurately for years in advance.

Early ideas and observations

By the eighteenth century, ships large enough to make the voyage to America and Australia were sailing along the Welsh coast. They traded from growing, commercially important ports: Liverpool, Newport, Bristol and Cardiff, which had big tides, shallow channels and exposed sandbanks at low water. Heavily-loaded ships could enter port only in a short window around high tide. Get the tide wrong and the ship could, at best, be delayed and at worst break its back on a rocky outcrop exposed as the tide fell.

Shipwrecks were common and

something had to be done. What was needed most was practical guidance for mariners in the form of accurate tide tables and guides to how the currents set at the entrance to harbours. This wasn't easy: although the cause of the tide was known at this time, the detail of how the sea responded to tidal forces was unclear. There were no accurate charts or tide tables.

In the second quarter of the eighteenth century, a pioneer who deserves to be better known undertook, virtually single-handedly, the complex task of preparing a set of accurate charts for the Welsh coast. Lewis Morris, born in 1701 on Anglesey,

21. High tides allowed large ships to enter Welsh ports but something had to be done to keep them afloat when the tide went out. The answer was to construct a lock gate at the entrance to the harbour, such as this one at the Queen Alexandra dock in Cardiff.

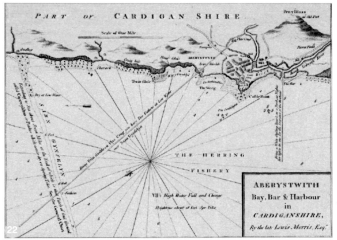

PART OF CARDIGAN SHIRE

ABERYSTWITH
Bay, Bar & Harbour
in
CARDIGANSHIRE,
By the late Lewis Morris, Esq.

THE HERRING FISHERY

VII: High Water Full and Change
Heightens about 18 feet Spr. Tide

were dry. On each of his charts he recorded the time of high water and the tidal range and I have reproduced his figures in the table below. The table follows Morris in giving the range in feet on a spring tide (how much it *heightens* in Morris's notation) and the time of high water on a day of a full or a new moon (*high water full and change*, Morris called it) in Roman numerals.

22. Lewis Morris's chart of the approaches to Aberystwyth (National Library of Wales).

began his great survey at Beaumaris in July 1737 and worked his way around the coast to Tenby by 1744 when the beginning of the war of the Austrian Succession stopped the work. His charts were published in 1748 and contain impressively accurate details about the tide.

Morris knew about the change in the tidal range and timing of high tide around the coast and recorded fine detail about the length of the flood and ebb, tidal eddies and the length of time that banks

Place	Heightens	High water full and change
Holyhead	24 ft	X
Caernarfon Bar	20 ft	IX
Nefyn	20 ft	VIII ¾
St Tudwal's	20 ft	VIII
Barmouth	14 ft	VII ¾
Aberdyfi	18 ft	VII ½
Aberystwyth	18 ft	VII ½
Cardigan	20 ft	VII
Newport, Pembs.	24 ft	VI ¾
Milford Haven	20-24 ft	VI
Tenby	30-36 ft	VI

The Tides of Wales

23. and 24. *Lewis Morris memorial near Brynrefail, Anglesey.*

Morris was aware of the relatively small tidal range in Cardigan Bay, between Barmouth and Aberdyfi (although we now would say that the minimum occurs closer to Aberdyfi than Barmouth). His observations of the times of the high waters, particularly the fact that high tide on Anglesey is about 4 hours after high tide at Tenby, accord well with modern data. In principle, these figures could have been used to predict the times of high water given the time of the moon's transit, but in practice, the delay between the moon being due south and the time of high water varies because of the effects of the sun's tides and other factors. Morris's figures would not have been good enough to make tide tables for everyday use.

The first accurate tide tables appeared in 1770 for the port of Liverpool and were produced by the Holden family, three generations of clergymen from Lancashire. These were some of the earliest, reliable tide tables produced in the UK and were a big improvement on previous efforts. The Holden family never revealed the method used to compile the tables, it is a secret they took to the grave, but it is likely that they calculated the shape of an ideal ocean covering the earth and pulled by the tidal forces of the moon and sun. They allowed for the variations in these forces with the earth-moon distance. That would have given them the relative sizes of the various rhythms of the tide. They could then have used observations of the actual tide at Liverpool to calibrate their calculations and give the actual heights and times of high water on any day. They had access to a good set of observations of Liverpool's tides; these had been made by William Hutchinson, the harbour master at Liverpool who recorded the times and heights of high waters day and night almost continuously

between 1764 and 1793. Members of the Holden family could then have performed the necessary calculations of the shape of the ideal ocean and the adjustments needed for their Liverpool predictions in their Lancashire rectory, with pencil and paper and a set of mathematical tables.

The Holden's method (if we have guessed it right) is no longer used for making tide tables. Instead, tides are predicted today by fitting curves to observations at a port and extrapolating the curves into the future. In their method, The Holdens needed to take into account the motion of the earth, moon and sun and then apply sound physical principles to see how the forces arising from this motion would shape the ocean. In important ways, their method was closer to the nature of the problem than the purely mathematical techniques favoured today.

2. Tidal Patterns

Tidal observations continued to be made along the Welsh coast through the nineteenth century as harbours developed and ships grew larger. Innovations such as automatically recording gauges and stilling wells allowed longer tidal records free from interference by wind-generated waves to be collected. By the 1920's there were enough observations on the coast and within the Irish Sea to enable accurate maps of the tidal behaviour for the whole sea to be drawn. The first people to do this properly were A.T. Doodson and R.H. Corkan of the Liverpool Observatory and Tidal Institute; they completed the job begun by Lewis Morris nearly 200 years earlier. Their work revealed the patterns that are weaved by Welsh tides. Although the times and heights of high waters change from day to day, there are fixed relationships (more or less) between the tide at different places. It is possible to represent these relationships on maps, using contours to show the nature of the tide in the same way that contours show the height of the land on Ordnance Survey maps or isobars represent pressure on weather maps. This information is interesting in its own right, but it can also be pressed into service to figure out how the tide works: the *reason* why the tidal patterns appear as they do. Once we know that, we can understand the tides not only in Wales, but have a fair stab at interpreting tidal behaviour anywhere in the world.

The time of high tide

A good place to begin is with contours showing the times of high tide. These can be drawn on a map if we select a reference, a zero on our clock to which tidal events can be related. A useful reference for this job is the time at which the moon appears due south in the sky. At this moment, the moon is crossing the longitude of the

1. *The time of high water in lunar hours after the moon's transit;*
2. *The tidal range in metres on an ordinary tide (half way between springs and neaps);*
3. *The maximum current speed (in m/s) on an ordinary tide.*

observer and is said to be making its *transit*. Since the motion of the moon is the principal cause of the tide we might expect that tide times will be related to the time of the moon's transit.

Observations confirm that this is the case and they show that high tide is seen first in Wales at Tenby on the south Pembrokeshire coast, about 5 hours and 40 minutes (5.7 hours)after the moon's transit. The high tide then proceeds up the west coast and, separately, eastwards into the Bristol Channel. It takes 4 hours for the tide to cross Cardigan Bay and reach Anglesey and then it covers the whole north coast of Wales more or less at the same time, within half an hour or so. The tide travels relatively quickly eastward from Tenby, reaching Newport in Gwent in about an hour and twenty minutes.

Relating tides to the motion of the moon is not particularly helpful unless you have a lunar almanac to hand. We normally reckon time by clocks which follow solar time. There are times, however, when solar time and lunar time coincide. On a day when it is new or full moon, the sun, moon and earth are in line. At new moon, the moon lies directly between the earth and the sun and the moon's transit must

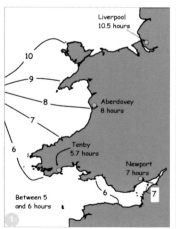
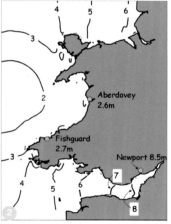
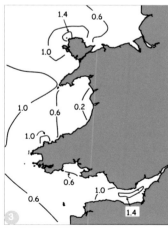

happen at the same time as the sun's transit, that is at noon GMT (although we can't usually see the moon at this time, because it is daylight). At full moon, when the moon lies on the opposite side of the earth to the sun, the moon makes its transit at midnight GMT. Happily then, on these days of full and new moon, the times of the moon's transit become the same as clock time in GMT. High tide at Holyhead, for example occurs at about 10 o'clock in the morning (and again at about 10 in the evening) on a day (or a night) with a new or a full moon. Lewis Morris knew about this useful rule and that's why he recorded the times of high tide at a port on days of new and full moon (he called it 'high water full and change').

In the table, I have listed the times, in normal clock time in GMT, of high tide on days of a new or a full moon for selected places around the coast (the times could refer to either the morning or the evening high tide). The times aren't exact for a number of reasons; nevertheless, they will be good to within half an hour or so most of the time.

The time of high water at new and full moon is sometimes called the tidal *establishment* of that place. The time of high tide advances from these times by an average of 50 minutes for every day after spring tides until, after 15 days, it is back to where it started and the cycle repeats. Seven days after springs, it is neap tides and the time of high tide has advanced by 7 times 50 minutes, or just under 6 hours. It is now low tide at the times shown in the table and so these are also the times of low water on a neap tide. Because the daily advance is the same for all places, the difference in the times from one place to another remains the same on any day. So, for example, high tide at Bardsey is always about two hours after high tide at Fishguard.

4. First in Wales, tidally speaking. Tenby on the south coast of Pembrokeshire.

Approximate mean times of high water on days of new and full moon and mean tidal range at various places around the coast

PLACE	TIME (GMT) hours and minutes	MEAN RANGE (m)
Newport, Gwent	7.15	8.5
Cardiff	7.00	8.0
Swansea	6.08	6.1
Tenby	5.48	5.3
Skomer Island	6.08	4.1
Fishguard	7.00	2.7
Aberystwyth	7.45	2.7
Aberdyfi	8.18	2.6
Pwllheli	9.20	3.2
Bardsey Island	9.00	2.8
Holyhead	10.00	3.6
Menai Bridge	10.15	4.7
Llandudno	10.36	5.4
Liverpool	10.54	6.0

The time of greatest tidal range, or spring tides, in Wales and much of the world actually occurs one or two days after new or full moon (this delay is called the *age* of the tide). The time of high water on a spring tide is therefore an hour or so after the times given in the table. The time of high water springs is important because this is the most likely time that flooding by the sea will occur at the coast, especially at the equinoxes when tides are greatest. Six hours later, or before, high water springs it is low water springs: the sea has retreated its furthest and it is time (for those who want to) to go digging for bait worms and looking for buried treasure.

The tidal range

Starting from Tenby, the range of the tide increases steadily travelling into the Bristol Channel, such that the great tidal ranges in the upper reaches of the channel are almost twice as large as those at Tenby. Moving up the west coast, the range first *falls* in Cardigan Bay before increasing again along the north coast of Wales. Travelling out to sea, that is westwards from Cardigan Bay, the tidal range decreases offshore and, remarkably, falls close to zero at Arklow on the Irish coast opposite Aberdyfi. Tidal ranges in Wales are increased by a factor of about 4/3 above their mean level on a spring tide (and decrease by a factor of about 2/3 on a neap tide). A mean range of 6 metres, for example will become 8 metres at springs and 4 metres at neaps.

Although the tides at Aberdyfi are small by Welsh standards, a visit to the town reminds you that they are still important. The water flows in and out of the Dyfi estuary at speed and a 'Time and Tide bell' has been installed on the pier, celebrating the legend of the submerged land of Cantre'r Gwaelod, whose bells – legend has it – can be heard ringing beneath the surface of Cardigan Bay.

5. The 'Time and Tide' Bell at Aberdyfi.

6. *Traeth Maelgwyn.*

Across the river from Aberdyfi lies Traeth Maelgwyn, or Maelgwyn sands, where according to legend, the powerful 6th century King of Gwynedd, Maelgwyn, invited his rivals to take part in a competition. All were to sit on chairs along the shore as the tide came in and the one who could remain in his seat longest could claim overall authority. According to the legend, Maelgwyn had prepared his chair so that it would float and so he won the competition.

We went to see the site of this tale on a hot sultry day in August when there was mist clinging to the hilltops and thunder rolling along the valleys. At the car park for the Ynys Las nature reserve a representative of Natural Resources Wales was welcoming visitors and warning about rip currents. Behind her stretched a great open space: the flat expanse of Traeth Maelgwyn running as far as the eye could see, with Aberdyfi twinkling on the far side of the river.

We wondered if there was a single grain of sand left from Maelgwyn's day. Families were strolling along the shore and a noisy speedboat was towing skiers on the river. The shore is a mixture of mud, sand, stones and, further along a great expanse of salt marsh. A salt marsh is a habitat that is periodically soaked in salt water with the tide. The plants – grasses and flowers - can survive temporary immersion in the sea. They, at least, have something in common with Maelgwyn's chair.

Tidal currents

Information about the tidal currents around the coast is available from tidal diamonds on Admiralty charts (tidal diamonds mark places where observations of currents over two or three tidal cycles have been made by a survey vessel). The fastest currents occur off headlands such as Strumble Head in Pembrokeshire, the

7. *Saltmarsh at the Dovey estuary with Aberdyfi in the background.*

north coast of Anglesey and in the Bristol Channel and also in sea straits such as the Menai Strait (which we will come to in the next chapter). There are weak currents in some of the bays, where the tidal streams

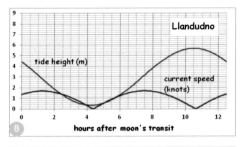

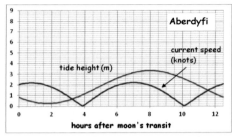

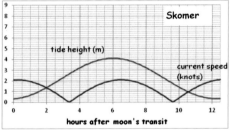

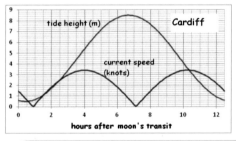

sweep across the mouth of the bay. There is a particularly large area of weak currents in Cardigan Bay.

The peak speed of the currents in the open sea, away from headlands and channels is about 1.4 m/s, or 3 miles per hour. This figure will increase to over 2 m/s (4.5 mph) on a spring tide. As we shall see in chapter 3, the currents in some of the narrow channels between offshore islands and the Welsh mainland can reach twice this speed. The speed of the flow in these

8. Plots of tide height and current speed at four locations around the coast. The scale on the left hand axis can be used for both height in metres and speed in knots.

channels is faster than that of the Gulf Stream, which is typically about 5-6 mph at its fastest. Tidal currents differ from ocean currents in an important way, though: they regularly reverse direction. If you sit on a tidal flow at the start of the flood, the current will accelerate, reaching maximum flood speed 3 hours later. The current will then slow down, and 6 hours after the start will reverse direction, carrying you back to where you started.

The relationship between currents at tidal diamonds and the height of the tide at a nearby port varies from place to place. All along the north coast, for example at Llandudno, slack water occurs close to the times of high and low water. On the west coast, there is a delay between high tide and the following slack water, so that the current is still flooding (flowing northwards) at high tide. At Aberdyfi, the delay is about 2 hours and at Skomer the delay has increased to 3 hours. At this south-west corner of Wales, fastest currents coincide with low and high tide; the exact opposite of the north coast. In the Bristol Channel, the pattern of the north coast is re-established, with slack water again coinciding with low and high tide. We will come to the reason for this behaviour later in this chapter.

Patterns that can be seen from space

Fast tidal currents are excellent mixers of seawater. Flowing backwards and forwards, especially over a shallow and rough sea bed, they are equivalent to a great food mixer swirling the sea around. The currents create a random motion, called turbulence, which stirs both horizontally and vertically. The variations in mixing from strong to weak currents create patterns in the colour, temperature and other properties of the sea which are big enough to be seen from earth-orbiting satellites.

The relatively weak tidal streams in Cardigan Bay create a special ecological niche not found elsewhere along the Welsh coastline. In the spring and summer the seas around the British Isles are warming. The sun's heat is stirred downwards from the surface by the turbulence generated by the tide, helped by the wind. This takes some effort because the surface water warmed by the sun is buoyant and energy is needed to mix it with the colder and denser water underneath. For most of Wales' coastline, the tides are strong enough (and the water shallow enough) for the surface heating to be mixed right down to the bottom and the sea has a uniform temperature in the vertical. It is said to be *vertically mixed*. In Cardigan Bay, however, the weaker tidal currents don't have the strength to mix the

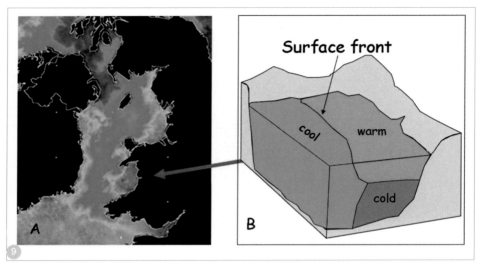

surface heating all the way to the sea bed and the water becomes layered, or *stratified*, with a warm surface layer heated by the sun and stirred by the wind lying on top of a cold layer which receives no direct heat from the sun. The stratification is helped by the fresh water flowing into the bay from rivers and adding further buoyancy to the surface layer. This area of stratified water fills most of Cardigan Bay during the summer months (although it can be temporarily destroyed by summer gales). At its edge, where the stratified water meets the vertically mixed water further out in the Irish Sea, there is a sudden

9. (a) *Thermal infra-red satellite picture showing the tidal mixing front in Cardigan Bay in early summer. Orange colours indicate surface temperatures of about 12.5 degrees and green about 10.5 degrees; (b) A 3D sketch of the structure of the front. The warm water lies over a deep layer of cold water with a temperature of about 9 degrees which cannot be seen by the satellite. (satellite picture: NEODAAS)*

transition in sea surface temperature, called a *tidal mixing front*, stretching across the mouth of Cardigan Bay.

The position of the front at the sea surface can be seen by satellites equipped with thermal infra-red sensors able to detect changes in temperature. The concentrated heat in the surface layer on the stratified side of the front makes warm surface waters. In Cardigan Bay this is particularly so in the north-east corner known as Tremadog Bay which, in summer, contains some of the warmest waters to be found along the Welsh coast. The warm water is ideal for sea bathing and is made even more attractive to swimmers because it is *clear*. Suspended particles, common in most Welsh waters, sink out of the surface layer of the stratified water and find it difficult to return. The change in particle concentration in surface waters creates a colour change, in addition to the temperature contrast at the tidal mixing front, green on the mixed side and clear blue on the stratified, inshore side.

The clear and warm waters, combined with sandy beaches made this coastline a popular tourist spot. Families in the 1950's and 60's enjoyed holidays in Butlin's holiday camp near Pwllheli, benefitting from the pleasant sea bathing in the conditions provided courtesy of the tide. Summer visitors still come to the area, attracted by the sparkling sea, golden sands and the spectacular backdrop of the Snowdonia mountain range. Cardigan Bay is also famous for its resident population of dolphins, one of the largest in the UK. The reason why the dolphins choose to live in the bay is uncertain, but the pleasant sea conditions may be a factor.

The idea that the tide can create fronts separating stratified from vertically mixed water was first proposed in the mid-1970s by two physical oceanographers, John Simpson and John Hunter, at what was then the University College of North Wales in Bangor. Tidal mixing fronts have subsequently been discovered in many places around the world: everywhere, in fact, in temperate latitudes and where there are large tides. They enhance the biological productivity of the sea and are sites of important fishing grounds. Simpson and Hunter made a bold move, making a prediction about where the tidal mixing fronts would be found. Their prediction was based on sound physics but at the time it was supported by a very limited set of observations. The prediction was soon to be tested in a way that they had not anticipated.

In the years following the launch of the first artificial satellite, Sputnik 1, a series of increasingly sophisticated meteorological satellites were put into orbit about the earth. The satellites travelled in a polar orbit, flying south to north (and then north to south) over points close to the poles. The gravitational pull of the earth's equatorial bulge made the orbit *precess*, or turn about its axis once a day, so that the satellite covered every part of the earth in 24 hours. The satellites were equipped with cameras to photograph cloud patterns during the day and infra-red sensors to detect the temperature contrast between clouds and clear sky at night.

The information from some weather satellites (notably those operated by the US National Oceanographic and Atmospheric Administration – NOAA) was freely available to anyone with a suitable receiver. In the UK in the late 1970s, two enterprising electronic engineers, Peter Baylis and John Brush set up a satellite dish on the roof the Electronic Engineering department at the University of Dundee and began generating pictures of weather patterns. Their receiving station was a mixture of the latest technology, home-made devices and opportunistic finds: the pictures were printed on facsimile machines obtained from newspaper offices in the city of 'jam, jute and journalism'. Dundee's pictures of weather patterns swirling across the Atlantic towards the British Isles were of such high quality that they became the official source of satellite imagery in the UK. Pictures of cloud patterns over the north-west Atlantic, now commonplace on television weather bulletins and in newspapers, first appeared on British TV about this time courtesy of the Dundee satellite receiving station.

The pictures became part of the story of Welsh tides because it was possible to adjust the contrast on the thermal infra-red images so that, instead of showing difference between clouds and clear air, they revealed the more subtle variations in the temperature of the sea surface. Carefully adjusting the contrast and focussing on the waters around the British

Isles, Baylis and Brush could see the positions of the tidal mixing fronts separating warm stratified water from cooler vertically mixed water. The position of the fronts exactly matched the theoretical predictions of Simpson and Hunter. It was a serendipitous meeting of a new idea about what the tides can do and the new technology needed to test that idea.

* * *

The makers of earth-orbiting satellites continued to develop new sensors, some of which were designed to measure the colour and brightness of the sea. The apparent colour of a water body can be deceiving. If you look at the sea at a shallow angle, for example from a beach or a cliff, you are most likely to see the colour of the reflected sky. The sea looks blue on a sunny day and grey on a cloudy one. A satellite looking vertically down sees something which is closer to the true colour of the water (you can see the true colour yourself by looking down into the water through a tube which cuts out surface reflections. The colour of the sea around the Welsh coast is a beautiful emerald green).

The colour is produced by thousands of tiny particles, mostly too small to be seen individually with the naked eye but which collectively colour the water and reduce underwater visibility. Some of the particles are living plant cells, called phytoplankton. They form the 'grass of the ocean' and, globally, produce about half of the planet's oxygen through photosynthesis. In Welsh coastal waters, though, the phytoplankton are usually heavily outnumbered by inanimate flakes of clay which often stick together in clumps called flocs. The flocs are loose aggregates of pieces of clay and bits of organic material joined together by sugary glues. They are easily broken up by an increase in turbulence made, for example, by stirring the water.

Although the flocs and other particles suspended in seawater are mostly microscopic, they are very good at reflecting sunlight and, when present in large numbers, create patches of bright water which can be seen by satellites fitted with sensors that collect reflected sunlight. One of the most prominent of these particle clouds, or patches of turbid water, lies north of Anglesey where there is an extended area of fast tidal streams creating enough turbulence to hold the particles in suspension in large numbers. As the tidal currents wax and wane with the springs-neaps cycle, Anglesey's patch of turbid water grows and shrinks. It is present all year although it is bigger in winter when storms contribute to the turbulent mixing.

Strong tidal currents are necessary to create these large turbid patches but they are not enough on their own. A patch of *anything* in the sea will gradually diffuse away unless it is continually replenished from a source. Diffusion (the natural spreading of a substance) will happen in any turbulent fluid and always works to even out gradients. Material in the sea diffuses from a place where it is plentiful to a place where it is scarce; inequalities are smoothed out. To maintain an area of high concentration, such as the turbid patch north of Anglesey, material needs to be pumped into the water at that place. The mystery is that there is no obvious source for the suspended particles in the turbid water north of Anglesey. There are no large rivers on this coast and the sea bed is composed mostly of pebbles. For this reason, these patches of highly turbid water have been called *isolated turbidity maxima* (or ITM).

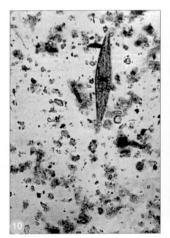

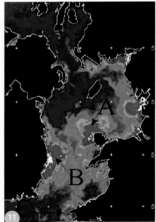

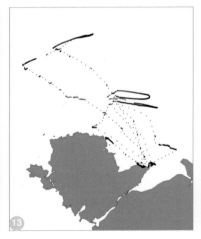

The first clue to how they might work came when it became possible to measure the size of the particles suspended in seawater using laser diffraction instruments. These measurements showed that, averaged over a tide, large particles were travelling into the turbidity maximum from the surrounding water and small particles were travelling back out again. The ITM sucks in large particles and then spits out small ones. What we think is happening is that the strong tide-generated turbulence within the ITM is able to break up the flocs into their constituent components – the individual pieces of clay and organic material –

10. *Particles suspended in seawater. The largest particle in this picture is a phytoplankton cell about 0.1mm long;*
11. *Sea surface brightness; areas of high brightness (and high particle concentration) are coloured red and marked with letters A, B and C; 12. Razorbills nesting on Puffin Island are tagged by the RSPB; 13. The birds follow the currents around Anglesey when they sit on the water at night.*
Photo credits: (10) Paul Smith,
(11) NEODAAS; (12) Derren Fox, RSPB, supplied by Ellie Owen, RSPB

making a cloud of many small particles which are easily mixed to the surface and create the bright patch that can be seen from space. The small particles diffuse out of the ITM and, as they move into the weaker turbulence in the surrounding water, they reform into flocs. These newly-created flocs then diffuse *back* into the ITM (where there is a scarcity of flocs) and the cycle is repeated. A balance is reached in which the mass of small particles diffusing out of the ITM is equal to the mass of larger flocs diffusing back in. The source of material that stops the ITM diffusing away is the surrounding water and the larger flocculated particles it contains. Indeed, it might be a necessary condition for the formation of an isolated turbidity maximum that the currents are strong enough to break up flocs.

The strong currents don't appear to deter seabirds, which are attracted to the north Anglesey coast in large numbers. The Royal Society for the Protection of Birds studies the behaviour of nesting seabirds by attaching small loggers to track their movement. The project is designed to provide information on the feeding habits of the birds but it has also provided information on the tides. The birds fly from their nesting ground on Puffin Island and rest on the sea overnight. The logger records their position every few minutes. When the birds are flying, the recorded positions are well spaced but when they rest on the water, their positions trace out smooth tracks. The tracks turn at the times when the tide is expected to turn and it looks as though the birds are acting as a good marker for the currents. On an overnight rest, the birds can travel up to 25 miles – carried by the tide.

Although the turbid water north of Anglesey looks bright from above, under the surface it must be rather gloomy. The large numbers of particles suspended near the surface scatter and absorb sunlight and make it difficult for light to penetrate far into the water. The murky waters provide a good hiding place for small fish who want to conceal themselves from predators (such as the seabirds tracked by the RSPB) attacking from above. Tim Whitton, a marine biologist at Menai Bridge, and his colleagues have been tracking the movement of shoals of small fish in the area with echo sounders placed on the sea bed.

The fish undertake a daily vertical migration, moving up towards the surface to feed at night and down to avoid predators during the day. If the water is particularly turbid, they are prepared to move closer to the surface and not go down quite so far. The turbidity fluctuates with the fortnightly springs-neaps tidal cycle and the average depth of the shoal (over a 24 hour period) responds to this; the fish move closer to the surface at spring tides when the currents (and turbidity) are highest. In winter, storms also contribute to making the water turbid and the tidal effect is muted, but in summer and autumn there is a regular fortnightly variation in the daily-mean depth of the fish. In this area of turbid water north of Anglesey both predators and prey are affected, in their own way, by the tide.

An explanation of Welsh tides

Mapping the behaviour of the tides around the coast is an important first step, but curiosity demands more. Why is the tide like that? How exactly does it work? What we are looking for when we ask these questions is a simple mechanism – a model – which is easily understandable, is memorable and which fits the observed facts. We do this all the time in normal

> 14. *The daily-mean depth of fish schools north of Anglesey change with the springs-neaps cycle, presumably as the darker water at springs makes the fish less vulnerable to predators such as seabirds hunting from above.*

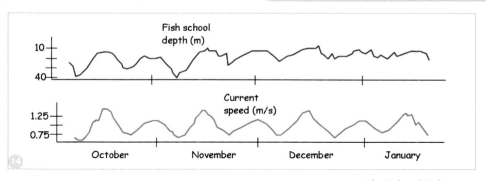

conversation. For example, the statement 'it is warmer today, spring must be on its way' contains an observation about the natural environment (it is warmer today) and an idea about why that might be so (experience tells us that there is a natural variation of air temperature with the seasons and we are entering a season when we expect the temperature to rise).

There is a balance to be struck when choosing a model to explain observations. A simple model is easily understandable but may not explain all the facts. A complicated model can be more like the real world but is hard to understand and it is difficult to learn anything new from it. The best models are ones that are no more complex than they need to be, match observations well enough and which tell us something new about the way that nature works. As Albert Einstein said: 'everything should be made as simple as possible, but no simpler'.

The tides around Wales can be understood by thinking of the water surface moving as a wave. We saw in chapter 1 that tide waves are created in the Atlantic by the gravitational pull of the moon and sun. These create subsidiary waves that travel across the continental shelf towards the south-west corner of Wales, where the wave divides, part travelling north and the rest east into the Bristol Channel. Let's first follow the wave that moves northwards across Cardigan Bay.

Any water wave, of which a tide wave is a specific example, consists of a series of crests separated by troughs. As the wave travels along, high tide occurs when the crest of the wave arrives; in a tide wave, this happens every 12 hours and 25 minutes. The speed of a tide wave across the sea bed just depends on the depth of water and, along the west and north coast of Wales, the speed is about 40 miles per hour, or 70 km/hr (coincidentally, about the same as the average speed of a car on the roads along these coasts). The distance from Skomer to Liverpool, as a wave travels, is just over 300km and the wave takes about four and a half hours to make the journey.

As the shape of the wave travels along, the water beneath the wave moves backwards and forwards. The water moves in the direction the wave is travelling at the crest of the wave and in the opposite direction at the trough. The speed of the

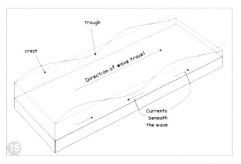

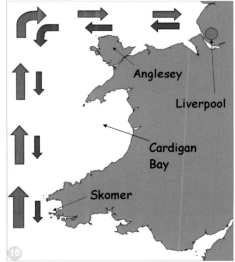

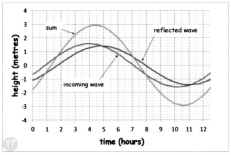

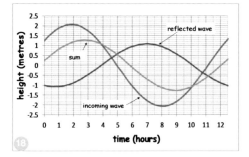

15. A tide wave travels up the west coast of Wales, is reflected off the coast at Liverpool and travels back, losing energy and height as it travels; 16. On the north coast, the two waves are in phase and, 17. add to produce a large tide simultaneously along this coast. On the west coast, the waves are out of phase; 18. The combined wave is smaller and it follows the incoming wave moving up the coast.

currents is much less than the wave speed, but the currents are essential for making the wave travel. The currents converging on a line ahead of the crest transfer the water so that the crest moves forwards. A wave like this, in which the crest travels over the sea bed and in which the currents are fastest at the crest and trough is called a progressive wave.

The progressive wave travelling up the west coast of Wales, across Cardigan Bay, takes a sharp right turn at Anglesey and travels to the English coast at Liverpool. At this coast, the wave is reflected and sent back the way it came. At a given distance from Liverpool, we can draw the tidal curve due to the incoming wave and that due to the reflected wave and add these together to see how the tide should look at that place. There is a time delay between the incoming and reflected waves, equal to the time it takes for the wave to travel from that place to Liverpool and back again (much in the same way as there is a delay in an echo reflected from the end of a cave). Let's start by assuming the incoming and reflected waves are the same size.

Near the reflecting coast (and so near Liverpool), the time delay between incoming and reflected waves is small and the two waves are said to be *in phase*. Their heights add constructively to create a wave with a large tidal range – equal to twice the range of the inbound wave at this point. The high water in the combined wave occurs at a time half way between the crests of the two constituent waves. Because the incoming and reflected waves are travelling in opposite directions, however, the currents in the two waves oppose each other and they cancel each other at high tide to create a high water slack. Moving away from Liverpool, the crest in the incoming wave arrives earlier and the crest in the reflected wave later; the waves move *out of phase*. The tidal range reduces, but the combined high water still occurs at a time half-way between the crests of the two waves. Since the incoming crest arrives at a set time before high water at Liverpool and the reflected crest arrives at the same set time after the high water at Liverpool, the high water in the combined wave happens at the *same time* as high water Liverpool. The time of high water as we move away from the coast remains constant and coincides with the time of high water at Liverpool.

Eventually, we reach a point where the high tide in the incoming wave coincides with the low tide in the reflected wave and vice versa. The waves are now exactly out of phase; they cancel each other out at all times and there is no tide. This happens at a place where the return journey of the wave to Liverpool and back takes six and a quarter hours – or the one way journey of a little over 3 hours. For a wave travelling at 70 kh/hr, the waves are exactly out of phase 210 km from Liverpool as the wave travels. This is the location of Aberdyfi. Travelling from Liverpool to Aberdyfi, the tidal range decreases steadily from twice the range of the constituent waves at Liverpool to zero at Aberdyfi. Moving further south than Aberdyfi, towards Skomer, the waves start to come back into phase and the tidal range increases again.

In reality, friction has an important effect on the height of the waves. The incoming wave reduces in height on its journey towards Liverpool and the reflected wave continues to lose height on its journey back from Liverpool. While we are still close to Liverpool, the two waves are similar in size and their sum behaves pretty much as we described in the last paragraph. The north Wales coast counts as being close to Liverpool and here high water occurs at about same time as at Liverpool, the tidal range is large but reduces with distance from Liverpool and slack water coincides with high tide. As we move around Anglesey to the west coast of Wales, however, we move into a different regime. The reflected wave here is weak and the incoming wave is predominant. The combined tidal wave behaves mostly like the incoming wave, moderated a little by the weak reflected wave. The time of high water gets progressively later moving northwards up the coast, following the incoming wave. The time of slack water moves forward so that the current is flooding at high tide, as befits a predominantly progressive wave. The reflected wave still has a residual effect, however, and at Aberdyfi where the two waves are exactly out of phase there is a minimum, but not a zero, in tidal range. The tidal range at Aberdyfi is equal to the *difference* in the range in the incoming and reflected waves at that point in their journey.

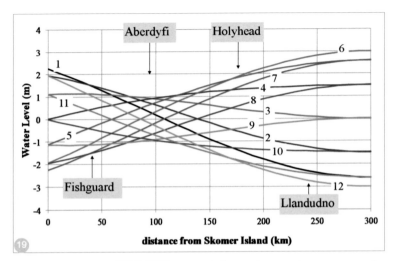

19. *The shape of the water surface between Skomer Island and Liverpool on a mean tide. The figures refer to times in hours relative to high water at Skomer, which occurs at hour 1. Skomer Island lies at the extreme left end of this figure (distance 0 km) and Liverpool at the extreme right (distance 300km). The position of some other locations along the coast is marked.*

The waves travelling in and out of the Irish Sea in this way are affected by the rotation of the Earth. The *Coriolis effect* deflects the moving water to the right in the northern hemisphere. The incoming wave presses itself against the Welsh coast and the reflected wave shifts across the Irish Sea and travels predominantly down the Irish coast. This transfer of energy westwards in the reflected wave supplements the effect of friction along the Welsh coast. It also means that the reflected wave is stronger on the Irish side. There is a place on the east coast of Ireland – at Arklow, opposite Aberdyfi - where the reflected wave is out of phase with the incoming wave and strong enough to cancel it at all times, creating a region of virtually no rise and fall of the tide (but also one of strong tidal currents). I remember once sailing into the harbour at Arklow, tying up on the harbour wall, heading for a pint or two of Guinness and returning a few hours later to find the ship at the same height on the wall when we returned. This was a very unusual experience for sailors used to Welsh tides.

A good model, as well as fitting the known facts, can tell us something we didn't know before. The tidal range at Liverpool, on an ordinary tide, is 6 metres and this is made by the sum of two equal waves – one incoming, one reflected – which must, therefore, have heights of 3m each at Liverpool. The tidal range at Aberdyfi, on an ordinary tide is 2.6m and, if our model is correct, this is the difference in the heights of the incoming and reflected waves at Aberdyfi. If we assume that the waves lose a fixed proportion of their height in travelling a set distance, then it is easy to show that the height of the incoming wave and reflected waves at Aberdyfi are about 4.5 and 2m respectively. The wave height is reduced by 50% (from 4.5m to 3m) on the journey from Aberdyfi to Liverpool and again by 50% (from 3m to 2m) on the way back. Now, the energy in a wave depends on the square of the height and so the reflected wave at Aberdyfi has only 1/5th of the energy of the ingoing wave. Fourth-fifths, or 80% of the wave energy is lost on its round trip to Liverpool and back. The picture of two damped waves travelling in opposite directions explains the nature of the tide and, by matching it to observations, we learn something new – how much of the energy in the tide is lost through friction.

It is interesting to see how the water surface behaves between Liverpool and Skomer as we move through the tidal cycle. This can be done by adding the two waves at a series of places at increasing distances from Liverpool and then plotting out the result. When we do this we can see that most of the time the water surface is sloping. The slope is impressive: up to five metres difference in water level between Skomer Island and Liverpool. A sloping water surface creates a horizontal force, called a pressure gradient force, which acts in the down-slope direction.

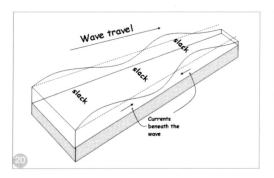

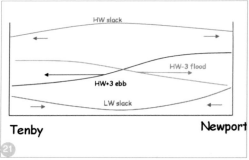

20. *The tide wave entering the tapered Bristol Channel and* 21. *the shape of the water surface and the currents at four stages of the tide.*

The role of this force changes during the tidal cycle. At the time of high tide at Liverpool, the pressure gradient force is decelerating the flood current and turning it into the ebb. At low water, the force – now acting towards Liverpool – reverses the current direction from ebb to flood.

Three hours before and after high water at Liverpool, the tidal currents are flowing at their fastest. They are not *changing* much at this time, however, and the accelerations are small. The slope is needed instead to drive the fast currents against the friction of the sea bed. At the time of maximum flood, the surface slopes down towards Liverpool to provide the necessary pressure gradient force to overcome the friction acting on the flow. During maximum ebb the slope is in the opposite direction, downwards from Liverpool to Skomer, to drive the water out of the Irish Sea.

* * *

The tides in the Bristol Channel are not so neatly explained by adding two damped waves travelling in opposite directions. The tide wave here behaves differently to the ones we have just been considering, mostly because the Bristol Channel is *funnel-shaped* and squeezes the wave, concentrating its energy. This makes big

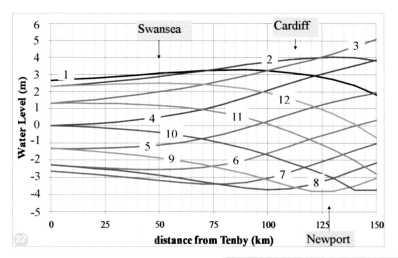

22. *The shape of the water surface in the Bristol Channel at hourly intervals on a mean tide.*

tides as the channel narrows. The resulting fast currents and shallow water make great frictional forces on the tide wave, so that there is not much energy left for the reflected wave.

Instead, a different kind of tide wave forms in the Bristol Channel. The sloping water surface between the crest and the trough of the wave creates a horizontal pressure force acting from the crest towards the trough, but the main job of this force is now to drive the currents against the strong bottom friction. Maximum flood current (that is flow in the direction the wave is travelling) moves forward from the crest to a point mid-way between the crest and the trough. The slope force then balances the friction force acting on the flood current. In fact, the whole current pattern shifts forward by a quarter-wavelength, so that the slack currents occur at times of high and low water. At these places in the wave, because there is no current, there is no friction and

no pressure gradient (and so no surface slope) is required to balance friction. In fact, because there is still some acceleration at the time of slack water (the flood changing to ebb), what is usually observed is that slack water occurs a little after high tide with the flood current coming towards its end at high water.

It is such a wave that travels along the Bristol Channel, although the wavelength is so long that only a portion of the wave fits in the channel at any one time. At high tide, the crest of the wave fills the channel

23. and 24. High and Low Tide at the Severn Crossing, the M48 bridge near Chepstow, looking towards England.

The Tides of Wales

and it is slack water in most places (although at this time, the doming of the surface creates a weak ebb flow near the mouth and a weak flood current at the inland end of the channel). Three hours later, the slope behind the wave crest fills the channel. The water surface now slopes up from Tenby to Newport and it is maximum ebb throughout the channel.

Three hours later again, it is low tide and slack water; the curve on the water surface once again creates weak currents at the two ends of the channel. Three hours later the slope before the next high tide fills the channel. This is the time of maximum flood and the surface slopes down from Tenby towards Newport.

The tide wave in the Bristol Channel

loses energy (and height) through friction and it is squeezed by the converging sides of the channel. This squeezing concentrates the energy and the shape of the wave depends on whether friction, or the squeezing, has the upper hand. In the River Thames in England, another example of a tapering estuary, these two processes just about balance each other out, so that the tidal wave travelling up the Thames keeps the same height; the tidal range at the entrance to the Thames estuary is similar to that in central London. In the Bristol Channel, the energy concentration effect is greater than the friction effect and the tidal range increases as the wave travels up the channel. The tidal range at Newport is 60% bigger than that at Tenby.

The sloping water surface in the Bristol Channel at any time creates a horizontal pressure gradient force acting down-slope. We saw earlier that in the case of the tide on the west and north coast, the work of this pressure gradient force changes during the tidal cycle: sometimes it is required to overcome friction and at other times to accelerate the flow. In contrast, the sloping water surface in the Bristol Channel is required, mostly, to drive flows against the effects of bed friction at all times.

*　*　*

The tidal range in the upper reaches of the Bristol Channel is the largest in the country and the largest in the world apart from a few select places in North America. On a big spring tide, the rise and fall of the tide in the section where the motorway bridges cross can be as much as 14m (46 feet). That's the same as the height of the walls of Caernarfon Castle. We went to see these big tides on a day when the tidal range at Newport was predicted to be 13.6m, just about as big as it can get. There are not many places where it is easy to get down to the shore on the Welsh side here. One spot where it is possible is on the Beachley headland a few miles east of Chepstow. Strictly, this is in England but we consoled ourselves with the thought that the water had been in Wales just a minute or so before. Most of the land here is Ministry of Defence property but there is public access to a car park beneath the M48 road bridge. There, we met a man walking his three dogs, including a very wet spaniel. 'Big tides today', he said, nodding. 'It's been a few years since the slipway has been completely covered'. He looked over the wall at the sea for a second and added 'and it's still coming in'. That was probably something his spaniel had failed to notice.

There is one further process that affects tides everywhere: the rotation of the earth. Moving objects on a spinning earth are deflected towards the right in the northern hemisphere and to the left in the southern hemisphere. This deflection is called the Coriolis effect and is the reason why winds blow *around* pressure systems in the atmosphere, instead of directly from high to low pressure. With a tide wave travelling down a channel, the Coriolis effect presses the wave against the right hand shore looking down the direction of wave travel. The right shore gets higher crests and lower troughs – a bigger tidal range – than the left shore.

Because of earth rotation, the tide wave travelling into the Irish Sea has a bigger range on the Welsh coast on its way towards Liverpool and a bigger range on the Irish coast on its way out again. The transfer of some of the reflected wave energy towards Ireland supplements the frictional losses on the Welsh side of the Irish Sea. It explains why the tidal range decreases moving westward towards Ireland. Along the Irish coast, the incoming wave is weaker, and the reflected wave stronger than on the Welsh coast. At the point where the waves are exactly out of phase, the two waves (incoming and reflected) are about equal in amplitude and add to make a point of no tide (this happens close to the port of Arklow). Earth rotation also affects the wave travelling into the Bristol Channel. The tidal range is a little greater on the English side of the channel than on the Welsh side opposite. Earth rotation only matters to things that move in the same direction for a significant part of a day. Tidal flows, which travel in the same direction for 6 hours are affected but the motion of water down a plughole, sadly, is not.

3. Sea Straits and Sounds

When a fast tidal flow is squeezed through a narrow channel, the result can be spectacular or frightening, depending on your point of view. Tides flowing through a narrow sea strait (also called a *sound*) can reach several knots and the channel has to be navigated carefully even by powered boats. The fast flows generate whirlpools and hydraulic jumps: exciting rapids that are sought-after by adventurous kayakers. These high-power channels are also obvious places to site tidal turbines to extract the energy in the tide and convert it into electricity.

Several of Wales's largest islands:

Skomer, Bardsey and Ramsey, for example, lie off peninsulas, or headlands. As the tidal streams approach these islands, the flow is squeezed through the channel between the island and the mainland. Water is, pretty much, an incompressible fluid and so if a flow of water is forced through a small gap it must speed up. We say that it is conserving the volume flow rate: the volume of water that passes a point in the flow each second is fixed. At each point in the flow, the current speed times the cross-sectional area of the flow is constant. If the cross-sectional area is reduced, the speed increases in proportion. The flow around the outside of the island also speeds up a little in order to keep up with the flow through the channel.

The channel offers resistance to the water that flows through it and water banks up on the upstream side of the

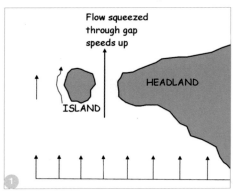

1. A tidal flow between an offshore island and a peninsula speeds up to conserve the volume flow rate; 2. Ramsey Sound, with Ramsey Island in the background.

The Tides of Wales

sound to drive the water through. The pressure gradient, or head of water, needed to drive the flow through a sound against the frictional resistance increases with the square of the current speed. If the required pressure head is greater than that available, no more water can flow through the channel. The water will then flow around the outside of the island instead For a 10km long, 20 metre deep channel, the water surface at the upstream end needs to be about 13 cm higher than the downstream end to drive a current of 1 metre per second. For a flow of 3 metres per second, the required level difference increases to 1.14 metres. Water flowing at that sort of speed, especially through a shallow channel with variations in depth and width, can generate some spectacular effects.

A hydraulic jump in Ramsey Sound

Ramsey Island snuggles up to the tip of St. David's peninsula, creating a sea passage less than 1 kilometre wide and about three kilometres long from south to north. The channel is further restricted by an archipelago of rocks, called the Bitches, stretching out at right angles from the Ramsey shore to within a few hundred

metres of the mainland. The place is a great magnet for kayak and surfing enthusiasts drawn to the set of fixed waves created as the already fast tidal flow accelerates through the gaps between the rocks.

It is exhilarating even to watch these skilled kayakers surfing on the face of the waves, with the water rushing beneath them with the power (and some of the sound) of a steam locomotive. Modern technology allows the participants to make videos using cameras on drones and these can be watched online. The tide flows at great speed through the gaps in the rocks (or, at high water, over the shallows on top of the rocks). Then, a little distance downstream, the fast-flowing but relatively flat water surface changes into a series of turbulent white-water waves which hold their position in the flow. The kayakers position themselves on the leading face of these waves so that the combined weight of the kayak and its occupant, acting down-slope, balances the drag of the water on

the kayak pushing it up the face of the wave. With the occasional paddle to keep the right orientation and position, the kayakers can hold their place with the water rushing beneath them.

The switchback ride that the kayakers are enjoying is an example of a natural phenomenon called a *hydraulic jump*. Flowing water has energy; in fact it has two types of energy: kinetic energy from its motion and potential energy which depends on the height of the water surface above some fixed reference level. As the water flows, the total energy (kinetic plus potential) is conserved, apart from losses created by friction.

3. A kayaker holding position on the face of a stationary wave, with the water rushing under his keel (photos: Preseli Venture Outdoor Activity Centre);
4. Kayakers preparing to ride the tide-generated stationary waves by the Bitches Rocks in Ramsey sound.

5. *The Bitches Rocks; 6. Skomer Island is one of the most important Puffin colonies in the UK; 7. Grey seals return to the safety of Ramsey's beaches in late summer.*

When a flow is squeezed through a gap it speeds up to conserve the volume flow rate. It gains kinetic energy at the expense of potential energy and the height of the water surface is reduced. The effect is exactly the same when air flows over an aeroplane wing: the faster flow over the top of the wing reduces the pressure and provides lift. In the case of water flowing over and through an obstacle such as the Bitches the reduction in pressure produces a step-down in water level as the water accelerates and a step-up as the flow slows down again at some point downstream. The mean level after the obstacle will not be quite as high as before because some energy is lost through friction in the fast flow.

At large spring tides when the speed of flow through the Bitches increases, the depression in water level becomes greater. There is a positive feedback mechanism operating here. The depressed water level restricts the cross sectional area; this speeds up the flow further which produces an even greater depression. Eventually a state can be reached where the flow is faster than the speed at which waves can travel on the water surface. When this happens all undulations on the surface, including the step-up, will be swept downstream to a position where the flow reduces (either because the channel widens or because of friction) sufficiently for the waves to hold their place in the flow. At this point the surface rises abruptly in a hydraulic jump. Any waves approaching the jump from the upstream direction will also be held up at this point and add to the energy in the jump.

The powerful waves in the jump are fixed relative to the sea bed; they are sometimes called stationary waves for this reason. The speed of waves travelling upstream is matched exactly by the speed of the current flowing downstream. The speed of a water wave depends on the water depth and the wavelength – the distance between crests. It

is waves with just the right speed – and so wavelength – which are held in the stationary wave. Shorter-wavelength waves with slower speed will be swept away downstream and longer waves with faster speed will make their way slowly upstream. For a current speed of 4 metres per second, or 8 knots, waves with a length from one crest to the next of 10 metres will have the right speed in all but the shallowest water and this distance – four or five times the length of a kayak – matches the length of the stationary waves seen in Ramsey Sound.

A flow of 8 knots would push against a typical kayak with a force equivalent to the weight of 4 kg. For a kayak and occupant with a combined mass of 80kg, a wave slope of 1 in 20 will make the component of weight acting down the slope match the drag on the boat. Waves with a wavelength of 10 metres would need to be 0.5 metres high; the waves forming behind the Bitches certainly have enough height. A skilled kayaker will find the right part of the wave slope to hold position in the super-fast flows.

The exact form of the jump depends on the conditions in the flow. Sometimes it is a steep wall of water with a great deal of turbulence on the downstream side of the jump. In other cases, such as at the Bitches, the jump takes the form of a stationary wave and is an example of an undulating hydraulic jump.

Human-sized hydraulic jumps in flowing water are relatively rare occurrences in nature, which is why the one in Ramsey Sound attracts such attention from enthusiasts. Small hydraulic jumps are much more common: they can be seen behind boulders in fast flowing streams, for example. You can also easily make one in a kitchen sink by running the tap at full speed. Water hits the bottom of the sink and spreads out radially in a shallow, fast flow. As it spreads out, the water slows down and, a few centimetres from the point directly beneath the tap, you will see a sudden

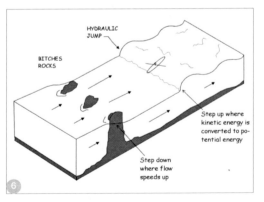

HYDRAULIC JUMP

BITCHES ROCKS

Step up where kinetic energy is converted to potential energy

Step down where flow speeds up

8. *A hydraulic jump created as fast tidal streams squeeze through the Bitches;*
9. *White water at the Bitches attracting flocks of sea birds.*

increase in the depth of the water created by a small hydraulic jump.

I made several trips to Ramsey Sound to watch the fun. Each time I was impressed as much as anything by the *sound* of the water. There's nothing quite like the noise of a powerful flow – the nearest I can come up with is the sound that a large locomotive makes as it approaches the platform. On my last visit, on a large spring tide in September, there were stationary waves and plenty of white water in the wake of the rocks. Seabirds were whirling above the flow, perhaps on the lookout for confused fish. I could see what all the fuss was about: this is one of the great spectacles that nature lays on for us. When I got back to the car park at St. Justinian's I chatted to a kayaker who'd paddled back faster than I could walk. It was his first time at the Bitches. 'How was it?' I asked. 'Marvellous', he said. 'Just like you see it in the pictures.'

Letters from an island

In 1927, the naturalist R.M. Lockley moved, with his family, to the remote island of Skokhlom in the south-western corner of Wales. During the second world war, he wrote a series of letters to his brother-in-law and friend, John Buxton, who had been captured and made a prisoner of war in Norway. The letters were designed to comfort his friend and remind him of a world outside the prison camp. They are mostly about the natural history of the area, but one of the letters was about the tides and currents in the channels between Skokhlom and Skomer Islands and the mainland.

Lockley observed and measured the tide in the area and in his letter offers good insight to the way they work. He measured the vertical movement of the tide at his island home by counting the landing steps that were covered between low and high water. The range, he notes, was 25 feet (7.5 metres) on a spring tide and no more than 12 feet on neaps, although in rough weather the 'waves splash another twenty to thirty feet' above the high water mark as they dashed against the landing steps.

He picked up knowledge of the currents in the sounds between the islands and the mainland during his regular trips to pick up supplies. 'I am enclosing six sketch maps' he wrote to Buxton, 'to illustrate six phases of the current between high and low water about these islands, which will perhaps give you a better idea of the regular changes of the tidal 'stream' as it is named on the charts.'

Lockley's sketches and ideas about what was happening are perceptive. He had realised that the currents in open water do not simply flow backwards and forwards; instead an arrow representing the current direction turns to point in different directions during a tidal cycle. The tip of the arrow traces out a curve, called a tidal ellipse, during the twelve and a half hours it takes to return to its original position. In the sketches, the sense of this turning is anti-clockwise.

He notes in his letter that some of the flows were driven entirely by local processes: the currents in and out of Milford Haven, for example, were necessary to make the tide rise and fall

10. Skomer Island viewed across Jack Sound; 11. Skokholm, home to the naturalist R.M. Lockley and his family.

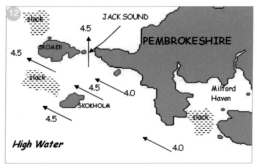

High Water

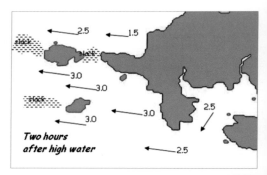

Two hours after high water

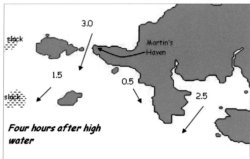

Four hours after high water

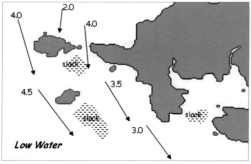

Low Water

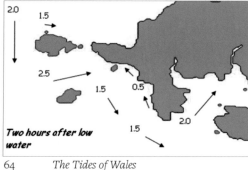

Two hours after low water

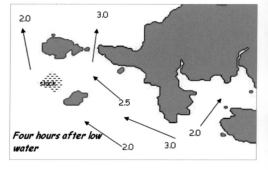

Four hours after low water

within the haven. Maximum flood current at the entrance to the haven happened when the tide was rising inside the haven and maximum ebb occurred when the tide was falling, with slack water in between these times. Elsewhere, however, the flows were driven by processes happening further afield. The flows around Skomer Island, for example, were driven by the forces that were filling and emptying the Irish Sea and so worked on a different rhythm to those in Milford Haven. Lockley also observed that the flows speeded up as they flowed around the flanks of an island and that there was an area of slack water, or weak currents, in the lee of the island. These are subtle effects which are a testament to his observational skills.

Lockley's sketches were based on his own experiences sailing his small boat in these waters and he also learned a lot from the local fishermen, who taught him that the 'first of the tide is always the best', that is you should launch your boat at the slack water before the current starts to flow in the direction you want to go. In practice this meant that he left Skokholm three hours before local high water and sailed north through Jack Sound during the north-flowing current and then returned from Martin's Haven three hours before low water to catch the south-going current. His sailing times were also dependent on the weather. 'At strong spring tides' he wrote, 'the current reaches between five and six miles an hour in the narrow part of Jack Sound and off Skokholm Head. Should the wind be against such a current the violence of the sea is very great, and Jack Sound at such a moment is a mass of short white waves through which no small boat could pass without filling.'

The idea of wind against tide is a common one; water waves made by the wind advance at a finite speed. If they meet a tidal current going in the opposite direction at the same speed, or faster, they can no longer advance. The waves behind catch up and the wave energy is concentrated in the region of fast currents, creating the turbulent conditions.

Today, visitors approach Jack Sound along the Marloes peninsula. Skomer

12. *The tidal flows around Skomer and Skokholm as reported by R.M. Lockley. Figures represent current speeds in knots.*

Island, the largest island in the group appears to be an extension of the peninsula until you get very close and see that it is separated from the mainland by a narrow sea strait, just a few hundred metres wide, with Skokholm lying off to the south. A small visitor centre at Martin's Haven has a video link to Skomer Island, so that visitors can watch the bird populations on the island in comfort and warmth.

Tidal whirlpools in Bardsey Sound

Bardsey Island lies off the western tip of the Llyn peninsula in north-west Wales and is separated from the mainland by a channel, about 3 kilometres wide, running in a south-east to north-west direction. The Welsh name for the island is Ynys Enlli, which translates as 'Island of the Currents': the area around the island has a reputation for its strong tidal flows. The currents in the centre of Bardsey Sound, according to the Admiralty chart of the region, reach 6 knots on a spring tide.

The mainland coast facing the island is known as Braich y Pwll, or 'Arm of the Pool' and this could refer to whirlpools in the region generated as the strong tidal flows rub against the coastline. Some years ago, there was commercial interest in drilling for gas and oil in the waters to the north of Bardsey and, as a result, a survey of the currents in the region was carried out. These observations shed new light on the whirlpools that form around the island on both the ebb and flood tides.

Measuring currents at sea is always a tricky operation, especially in strong flows which can drag moorings fitted with current meters. The currents around Bardsey were measured by a research vessel equipped with an acoustic current meter that could operate continuously while the ship was underway. A ping of sound is sent into the water; the echo which returns from the water has a change in pitch, a Doppler shift, which depends on the speed of the water relative to the ship. The ship's speed over the ground can also be determined from the frequency change in the echo from the sea bed; combining these figures gives the speed of the water over the ground. There are several benefits to measuring currents in this way: there is no need to stop the ship and the

13. Bardsey Island viewed from Braich y Pwll.

measurements do not interfere with the flow itself. Moreover, there is a series of echoes from different depths below the ship and so the variation of current with depth can be measured.

The results of the survey showed that there was an area of slack water in the lee of the island which could be resolved into a pair of oppositely-rotating whirlpools formed during the time of fastest flows. These whirlpools spin up in the lee of the island while the current is fast and then, as the tidal currents slow down towards slack water, the whirlpools continue to spin under their own momentum. As the tide turns, the whirlpools are squashed against the island and disappear, but a new pair of tide-generated whirlpools then springs up on the opposite side of the island.

Whirlpools, or eddies, like this could play an important role in trapping pollutants close to the island and it would be useful to know more about them. They are created by the island standing in the way of the tidal flows. The current speeds up as it curves around the flanks of the island in order to keep up with the offshore flow which is travelling in a straight line. The flow then slows down to its original speed on the downstream, or lee side, of the island. To achieve these accelerations and decelerations there are changes in water pressure: the water pressure and water level are low on the flanks of the island. The principle of energy conservation can be applied here, as it was to explain the hydraulic jump in Ramsey Sound. If water speeds up and its kinetic energy increases, then the potential energy falls in order to conserve total energy. The depression in sea level on

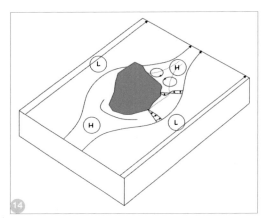

14. *Whirlpools forming in the lee of an island in a tidal flow. The letters H and L mark places with high and low pressure.*

the flanks of an island 10km across in a 1 m/s flow will be about 5cm.

The water closest to the island is also slowed down by friction with the island itself and with the sea bed in the shallows near the island shore. This creates a gradient of velocity, increasing away from the island. This part of the flow, in which the velocity is affected by the proximity of the shore, is known as a boundary layer. Now, the increase in pressure from the island flanks to the lee side of the island serves to decelerate the flow which has been speeded up on the flanks. But, the friction in the boundary layer is also decelerating the flow; as a result there is an enhanced deceleration close to the shore. Some of the water closest to the shore in the boundary layer is slowed to a complete stop and is then reversed. A region develops in which the flow is in the opposite direction to the mean flow further offshore. If we subtracted the mean flow, we would see a spinning motion in the water, clockwise on one side and anti-clockwise on the other side of the island. As this spinning motion enters the area of slack water on the lee of the island it creates two eddies rotating in opposite directions.

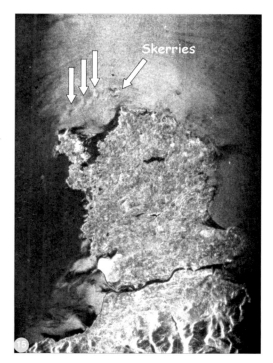

15. Satellite radar image of Anglesey during the ebb tide. Eddies can be seen shedding off the Skerries in the top-left of the picture. Three eddies are marked, separated by a distance of 3.4 km (2.1 miles).

These eddies are probably common features of islands in fast tidal currents, although they are rarely observed. If the flow is fast enough, the eddies can become detached from the island and carried away downstream by the flow. New eddies are created and a series of alternatively clockwise and anti-clockwise whirls appears in the island wake. This probably happens in the particularly fast flows past the small group of islands known as the Skerries to the north-west of Anglesey. Radar images of these islands, returned from orbiting satellites, show a series of dark and bright patches stretching away from the island on the downstream side. These are probably caused by variations in surface roughness as the wind interacts with the surface current in the spinning eddies.

Tides in the Menai Strait

Anglesey is Wales's largest island and it is separated from the mainland by the country's longest and narrowest sea passage. The Menai Strait, Afon Menai in Welsh, runs south-west to north-east for 25 km and varies in width from a few hundred metres to several kilometres. At its narrowest point it is crossed by two spectacular bridges, Telford's road suspension bridge, opened in 1826 and Stevenson's Britannia Bridge, opened in 1850 originally as a railway bridge but now providing both a road and rail crossing.

The strait offers sheltered conditions for sailing boats but the tidal flows are strong and turbulent and need to be

16. Map of the Menai Strait;
17. An aerial photograph of the two bridges across the strait (photo: David Roberts);
18. The training ship HMS Conway (originally launched as HMS Nile in 1839) was caught by the tide in the Menai Strait in 1953 and subsequently wrecked.

treated with caution. Horatio Nelson knew that the tides here demanded respect. In 1953, a warship with a design that would have been familiar to Nelson was wrecked in the strait after getting into difficulties with the tide. *HMS Nile* was a 2-deck 90-gun second-rate ship of the line, launched at Plymouth naval dockyard in 1839. She served in the Crimean War before being converted to a training vessel in 1876. She

was renamed *HMS Conway* and was based originally on the River Mersey, but amidst fears that she might be damaged in the Blitz, she was moved to the Menai Strait in 1941.

In 1953, the old ship was being towed to Birkenhead for a refit and making the passage through the Swellies, the notorious section of the strait between the bridges. The two tugs that were towing her could not make headway against the adverse, strong flows. An eddy turned the ship broadside on to the flow and she ran aground with her bow section on a rock and her stern still floating. As the tide fell, the weight of the sinking stern forced the ship's timbers apart and she flooded on the next rising tide.

The tidal flows in the strait can confuse because they continue to flow at high and low water and at times can be flowing in different directions in different parts of the strait. Essentially, the flows are driven by the difference in water level between the two ends of the strait. The horizontal pressure gradient force created by the resulting slope on the water surface accelerates the water and also serves to overcome frictional resistance on the flow.

Much of the time the two biggest forces are the pressure gradient and friction; the slope on the sea surface drives the flow down-slope against the friction of the sea bed.

The tidal range is greater at the Beaumaris end of the strait. This is because Beaumaris is closer to Liverpool and, as we saw in the last chapter, the tidal range on the north coast of Wales increases towards a maximum at Liverpool. At high tide, the water surface slopes down from Beaumaris to Caernarfon; the flow at this time is down-slope and is directed towards Caernarfon. Six hours later, at low tide, sea level is lower at Beaumaris and the water flows towards this end of the strait. This simple picture accords with what we see in the strait at low and high tide: there is a flow towards the south-west at high tide and a flow north-eastward at low tide. Now, the frictional resistance is greatest at low water when the effect of the flow rubbing against the sea bed is most keenly felt. The pressure gradient, however, is the same in the two directions and so the flow reaches a greater speed at high tide when it is flowing towards Caernarfon. Averaged

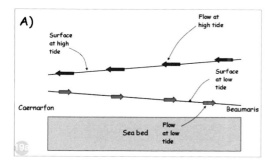

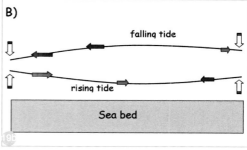

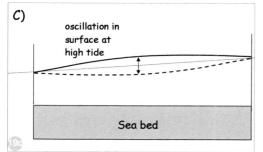

19. a) *The tide in the Menai Strait is driven by the sloping water surface created by the larger tidal range at Beaumaris; b) Inertia creates a dome in the water surface during the falling tide and depression on the rising tide; c) The relaxation of the dome around high tide can produce a temporary oscillation (a transient seiche) with largest amplitude in the middle of the strait. The size of the oscillation has been exaggerated in this sketch.*

over a tidal cycle, there is a net (or residual) flow directed towards the southwest. Observations show that this residual flow amounts to several kilometres per day. The strong tides and the residual flow provide excellent flushing mechanisms for removing pollutant from the strait.

Because the Menai Strait is long and narrow, the water flowing in and out cannot fill and empty the centre of the strait quickly enough for it keep up with the tide at the ends of the strait. Sea level in the centre lags a little behind that at the ends. On a rising tide, the surface in the centre is depressed below a straight line connecting the levels at Caernarfon and Beaumaris. On a falling tide the water level in the strait is slightly domed and higher in the middle than it is at the two ends. The curvature in the shape of the water surface means that the water can be flowing in different directions in different parts of the strait. For example, during the falling tide, 3 hours after high tide, water flows simultaneously out of both ends of the strait, squeezed out by the high pressure like toothpaste from a tube. On the rising tide, the low pressure in the centre sucks water in from the two ends.

Tide-made seiches and a double high water

One of the delightful things about flowing water is that it can come up with surprises. As high tide is approached and the rate of rise slows down, the flows fill the depression in the centre of the Menai Strait and the inertia of the inflowing water causes an overshoot. The shape changes from being low in the centre to being high in the centre. For a short while,

20. *Plas Newydd, home of the Marquess of Anglesey.*

The Tides of Wales

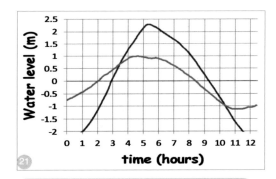

21. *Tidal curves at Plas Newydd at spring tides (blue) and neap tides (red) when a double high water can be seen.*

this change can cause an oscillation in the water surface. The movement is like that of a violin string, with the ends fixed by the sea level in the open sea and the middle part going up and down the most. The technical name for this kind of wave motion, in which the wavelength is set by the size of the water body, is a *seiche*. Seiches were first observed on Lake Geneva in Switzerland (the word 'seiche' is Swiss French dialect for 'swaying back and forth'). The analogy with the bow string is complicated by the fact that, in the strait, the ends continue to rise and fall with the

tide (so it's like a vibrating violin string with the violinist sitting down and standing up).

For a water body with the length and depth of the Menai strait, we would expect the period of this seiche motion to be about two and a half hours. This motion is superimposed on the tide and is most apparent in the centre of the strait, the section by Plas Newydd, the stately home of the Marquis of Anglesey.

The seiche doesn't last for long, just for an hour or so around high tide (there is barely time for a complete oscillation). As the water level falls and friction becomes more important as the water shallows, the seiche is quickly damped down: it is called a transient seiche. If you've ever shaken the creases out of a bed sheet by swinging it up by its corners you might have noticed the temporary oscillation that is set up as the sheet reaches its highest point. The effect of the transient seiche on the tide in the centre of the Menai Strait is to change the shape of the tidal curve at high water: it becomes sharply pointed. Very occasionally, the regular tide is small enough and the seiche large enough for the oscillation to create a dip after the high tide and then a small second high water about an hour after the first. Such *double high waters* are extremely rare. There is a well-known one at Southampton on the south coast of England and there are a few other documented examples world-wide. The Southampton double high water occurs regularly at spring tides and makes an extended period of high tide which has been important in the commercial development of the port. The double high tide in the Menai Strait is different: it is much smaller and less reliable than that at Southampton; it appears at neap tides when the regular tide is smallest and the frictional damping on the seiche is least. Nevertheless, the fact that it occurs at all means that Wales can lay claim to possessing this rare tidal phenomenon.

Tides and the flocculation of suspended particles

It is a common (and many would say unfortunate) feature of tidal waters around the world (Wales being no exception) that they are *murky*. The fast tidal currents, and the turbulence they produce, lift and hold tiny flakes of mud and other material in suspension, carrying them along with the flow. The particles colour the water, make it difficult for sunlight to penetrate to any depth, and reduce underwater visibility for animals, human and marine. Although it can be a nuisance, the turbidity created by tidal stirring is a completely natural process and doesn't necessarily indicate the presence of pollution.

As we noted in the last chapter, small particles suspended in salt water have a tendency to stick together in groups, called flocs. The flocs are held together by sugary glues naturally present in the water (especially in summer), but they are fragile structures easily disrupted if disturbed (for example, if a water sample is collected to look at under a microscope). The best way to see the flocs is with underwater cameras set up to magnify the individual flocs without disturbing them. Most flocs are too small to be seen by the naked eye although in the deep ocean they can grow quite large and, as they fall towards the ocean floor, look a little like snowflakes (they are, in fact, called marine snow). Flocculation is induced intentionally in water treatment plants because the larger flocs settle out more quickly than the individual pieces which make them up.

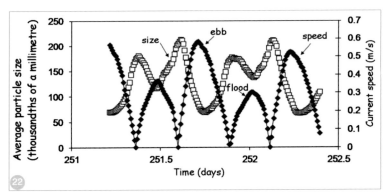

Turbulence created by the tide causes particles suspended in the sea to collide with each other and, if they are sticky enough, they clump together to make a floc. Turbulence is also able to tear the flocs apart, especially if they grow above a certain critical size. There appears to be an equilibrium size for the flocs at which their growth is just balanced by their breaking up. The equilibrium size depends on the level of turbulence and so, in a tidal stream, on how fast the water is flowing. We might expect, therefore, that the size of suspended flocs will change over the course of a tidal cycle as the current speeds up and slows down.

When a laser beam is aimed at a collection of suspended particles it creates a pattern, called a diffraction pattern, which depends on the diameter of the particles. This principle can be used to measure the size of the particles in suspension, without having to collect a water sample and risk disrupting the flocs. Measurements with such an instrument placed on a frame on the bed of the strait near Plas Newydd revealed something

22. *Particle size and current speed in the Menai Strait;* 23. *The Menai Strait looking towards the west, with the Rivals in the background. Plas Newydd is on the right bank in a gap between the trees where the channel is curving round to the left. Photo: David Roberts*

The Tides of Wales

really quite remarkable. As the current speed changed with the tide, the average size of the particles in suspension also changed; the particles were largest when the currents were weak and smallest when the currents were strong. The average particle size changed, every tide, by a factor of 3 or more (from about 0.07mm to 0.2mm and back again) as the current speed increased and decreased. Even though flocs are expected to behave like this, it is a surprise to see it happening, in reality, so clearly. The particles in the strait are growing and shrinking with the tidal streams, four times a day.

The currents in the strait are a little faster in the ebb direction, and the particles duly become smaller during the ebb. There is also a difference in size on the two slack waters: particles are smaller on the slack after the ebb than on the slack after the flood. Some of these changes can

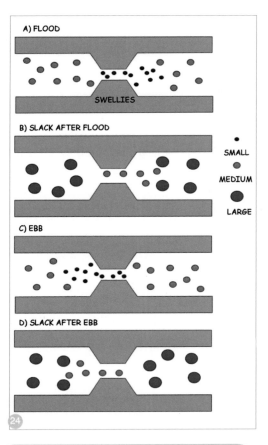

2. *Sketch of the processes affecting the size of flocs passing through the Swellies.*

be explained by the effect on the flocs of the turbulence generated at the observing site. As the current speed picks up, it breaks up the largest flocs into smaller pieces, reducing the average particle size. As the current slows, the small pieces reform into flocs. This is something akin to what we saw with the isolated turbidity maxima in chapter 2. The total mass of matter in suspension probably stays about the same, but the distribution of sizes, and the average size, changes with the tide. Added to this local effect is the fact that the current will bring particles from other parts of the strait to the observing site. In particular, the central part of the strait (the Swellies) between the two bridges is narrow and shallow; here the currents are particularly fast and turbulent. As particles pass through the Swellies, the breaking-up process will be at its strongest and we can expect that here the particles will be smaller than anywhere else. On the ebb flow, a wake of smallest particles is created streaming from the Swellies towards the south-west. At Plas Newydd, which is located 2 miles south-west of the Swellies, this wake will further reduce the size of the particles seen on the ebb. As the current weakens to slack-after-the-ebb these particles don't have time to grow as much as at the slack-after-the-flood before the current picks up again.

The strange business of particles flocculating is not confined to Welsh waters or even to the oceans of earth. The European Space Agency's Rosetta Mission sent a spacecraft for a close-up encounter with the comet 67P/ Churyumov-Gerasimenko. The ice and dust particles in the comet's tail were observed to be flocs: they broke on the spacecraft's collector like snowballs on a window-pane. Indeed, flocculation probably kicks off the formation of planets around new stars. It is a fundamental process, important to the way our solar system and other planetary systems are created. And yet, at the moment, no-one is quite sure how the flocculation and break-up of particles works, exactly. Space missions are expensive. Observing the flocculation of particles in the sea would be a much easier way to study this poorly-understood process.

4. Tides in Estuaries and Rivers

Wales is blessed with many beautiful estuaries that owe their good looks in part to the fact that they are swept clean, twice a day, by the tide. At low tide, there is an expanse of mud and sand cut through in places with shallow channels carrying brackish water to sea. The exposed banks at this time are important feeding grounds for sea- and wading birds: seafood restaurants that open for business twice a day. As the tide rises in the open sea, water is forced into the estuary – first up the channels and then over the tops of the banks, the very highest reaches of the banks becoming covered as high tide is approached and the currents go slack in anticipation of the start of the ebb flow. Welsh estuaries re-invent themselves each time the tide goes out and comes back in, expelling the day's accumulated rubbish and importing clean sea water.

The currents associated with the rise and fall of sea level in an estuary can be fast; the speed is governed by the need to fill the estuary in the time allowed between low and high water. An estuary with an area of 10km^2 and a tidal range of 5 metres imports fifty million cubic metres of water in six hours (at a mean rate of 2300 m^3/s). The volume of water that flows into the estuary between the low and the high tide is known as the *tidal prism*. If the tidal prism passes through an estuary entrance 1km wide and 5 metres deep, the average flow speed during the flood tide will be half a metre per second or one knot; peak flow speeds will be greater than this value by about 50%.

Estuary tides

The tide in an estuary is driven by the rise and fall of water level at the seaward-end, or mouth, of the estuary. As the tide rises and falls in the open sea, it creates a slope on the water surface either into or out of

1. A typical Welsh estuary: the Taf at low water, seen from Dylan Thomas's boathouse; 2. and 3. Two beautiful estuaries. The Glaslyn at Porthmadog with the mountains of Snowdonia in the background and the Mawddach viewed from the Barmouth railway viaduct.

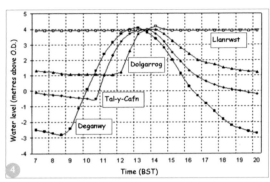

the estuary. On the rising tide, the surface slopes down into the estuary making a pressure gradient force directed into the estuary and the reverse is true on a falling tide. The river also makes a contribution to the flows but this is usually small compared to the tide. Typically, rivers add fresh water to Welsh estuaries at an average volume flow rate of less than 10m³/sec (although it can be much higher than this for short times during periods of high rainfall). In comparison, the volume flow rate due to the tide is typically several thousand m³/sec.

Observations of tide height at different places in an estuary show that the nature of the tide curve changes with distance inland. The tide curve in an estuary is asymmetrical: the duration of the rising tide, from low to high water, is less than that of the falling tide. The asymmetry becomes more marked with distance inland. The mean water level also increases with distance inland. As an example, we can refer to some measurements made in the Conwy by D.W.Knight and J.R.West of the University of Birmingham.

In a short estuary like the Conwy (and all Welsh estuaries), the current floods (or flows inland) when the water surface inside the estuary is rising and it ebbs when the surface is falling. At Deganwy, near

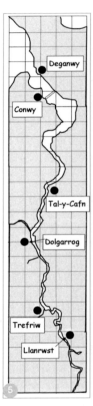

4. Tide levels at spring tides at different places on the Conwy measured by Knight and West; 5. Map of the Conwy. The squares are one kilometre on a side.

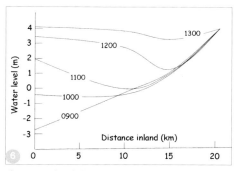

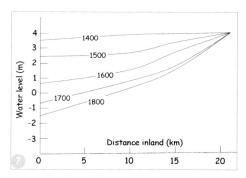

the mouth of the Conwy, the flood lasts for four and a half hours and the ebb for nine hours, twice as long. At Dolgarrog, 15 km inland from the mouth, the duration of the ebb is five times that of the flood. Since roughly equal volumes of water enter and leave the estuary on the ebb and flood tide, the fact that the flood is shorter in duration means that it must also be faster. The difference between the ebb and the flood tide in an estuary has important consequences. The fast flood tide carries more mud and sand into the estuary than can be removed by the slower ebb. As a result, estuaries fill with mud, creating the banks that we see at low tide. Estuaries that are seaways for large ships need to be dredged to remove the sediment brought in by the tide.

6. The shape of the water surface in the Conwy estuary on the flood tide and 7. on the ebb. The time of each profile is marked.

The observations of the tide in the Conwy can be used to draw the shape of the water surface at different times during the tidal cycle. At low tide, the river surface slopes down from Llanrwst towards the sea by 7m in 21km, a gradient of 1 in 3000. As the tide rises at the estuary mouth, it gathers itself together and surges inland up the estuary. The steep slope of the surface makes the tide rise rapidly as the surge passes a fixed point on the river. This surging motion is a result of the fact that the tide is driving water uphill. As the water flows uphill, it is gaining potential energy: extra force is needed to do the work, in the same way that you have to push harder to roll a heavy ball up a hill. The extra force is provided by the steeper slope of the water surface at this time. As the high tide reaches the upper parts of the estuary, sea level is starting to fall at the mouth. During the ebb tide, the surface relaxes back to low water.

The surging passage of the flooding tide and gentle sinking of the ebb are characteristic of the shallow estuaries with a mountainous hinterland that we have in Wales. You can see a similar effect at the water's edge on a sloping beach. Breaking waves advance up the beach in a surging motion and then the water flows back downhill towards the sea meeting the next incoming wave as it does so.

Tidal bores

When conditions are right, the steep slope of the surface in the advancing tide in an estuary can form into a tidal river bore. A tidal bore is the most dramatic and spectacular of tidal phenomena, seen on only a small number of estuaries worldwide. It is an example of the hydraulic jump that we came across in chapter 3: a rapid rise in water level often accompanied by a train of waves. Unlike the stationary hydraulic jump in Ramsey Sound, in which the waves are kept in place by a fast current flowing in the opposite direction, a tidal bore is a moving hydraulic jump which travels up the estuary driven by a rapid rise in the water surface behind it.

Before the bore arrives, the river is flowing sedately towards the sea. When the bore arrives, the direction of flow turns abruptly and the water flows rapidly inland and the water level quickly rises. Bores often make a roaring sound – called the rumble. The rumble heralds the approach of the bore, often before it can actually be seen. Sometimes, the bore will be a steep wall of turbulent water advancing up river but, more commonly in Welsh estuaries, it takes the form of a train of waves known as an undular bore. It is possible to surf large bores, such as that on the Severn in Gloucestershire in England, for several miles inland. Welsh tidal bores

8. The tidal bore on the River Dee. (photo Martyn Roberts)

are not usually large enough for surfing but they are still very exciting to watch, particularly so as some of them are elusive and take some tracking down.

The River Dee has the most reliable river bore in Wales. The best place to see it is in the canalised section between Connah's Quay and Saltney. Arrive before local low water and wait for the tide to come in. The exact time of arrival depends on the height of the river and wind conditions as well as the tide, so it is best to be early. Sometimes, if the river is high after heavy rain, there may be no bore at all. The bore on the river Dee travels faster than walking pace but it is possible to keep up with it on a bicycle and there is a good cycle track along this part of the estuary. The best time of year to see the bore is when the tides are largest: at spring tides near the equinoxes in March and September.

It is probably fair to say that the exact conditions needed to make a tidal bore in a river are not properly understood. A large tidal range at the estuary mouth is certainly an essential ingredient. There are no bores (apparently) on the rivers in west Wales where the tide is relatively small. But, a large tidal range is not enough on its own. A funnel-shape to the estuary also helps to concentrate the tidal energy and the slope of the river bed is important. What happens then probably goes something like this. The rising tide at the estuary mouth sends water flowing into the estuary. The inflowing water turns the direction of flow from ebb to flood and raises the level of the surface of the estuary. The point at which this happens can be thought of as the leading edge of a tide wave travelling up the estuary.

Now, there is a limit to the speed at which a wave can travel over a water surface. This depends, amongst other things, on the water depth. Waves can travel faster in deep water. If the estuary is too shallow to let the incoming tide wave advance at the speed dictated by the rising tide at the mouth, there is a build up of water which increases the depth to a level where the wave *can* advance at the required speed. At the leading edge of the tide wave, there is then a jump in the water level, often accompanied by a train of waves which are travelling into the estuary as fast as the water depth allows them.

The waves associated with an undular bore are called *whelps*. If the bore encounters a bend in the river, the whelps carry on, pretty well, in a straight line. They collide with the bank, reflect off it and travel at an angle across the river, adding to the generally chaotic conditions created by the bore. It is possible to simulate the formation of a bore in a channel with the water level rising at one end, by solving on a computer the equations that govern the flow of water. The leading edge of the wave quickly steepens and creates a sudden jump in water level followed by a series of small whelps.

If there has been a lot of rain and the river level is high, the tide wave can advance more quickly and a tidal bore may not form, which explains why bores don't always occur in wet weather. Whatever the exact physics of tidal bores, they are one of the most exciting tidal phenomena to behold and are well worth taking the trouble to seek out.

Tidal bores have been photographed on the Taf in Carmarthenshire and on the Usk at Newport in Gwent. There is also a report of a possible sighting of a bore on the Loughor estuary near Swansea. Each of these estuaries has the right conditions for bore formation: the estuaries are funnel-shaped and have a large tide at the mouth. I made several fruitless visits to the Taf in the hope of seeing the bore. There are some essential facts that bore-chasers soon pick up. One is that the bores don't keep a tight schedule; it is essential to turn up early in case the bore decides to do the same. This

9. *Computer simulation of the development of an undular bore on a river. As the tide rises on the left, it tries to send the leading edge of a wave into the river faster than a wave can actually travel. The water level builds up and a bore is formed.*

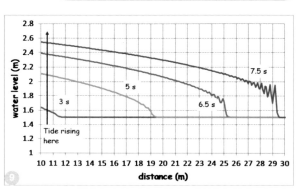

often means long waits in dreadful weather and strange looks from passers-by. If the tide has turned and water is flowing into the estuary, you are too late; you might as well go home or try your luck higher up the river. Big spring tides near the equinoxes and a period of dry weather (not an easy combination in Wales) encourage bores to put in an appearance.

On my final and only successful trip to see the Taf bore I stood one grey afternoon in mid-March on the footpath by Dylan Thomas's writing shed in Laugharne, chatting to the dog-walkers and waiting for the tide to turn. It turned, on time, at 4.05pm. There was no bore but, as I'd noticed before, the turn of the tide does change the appearance of the estuary in subtle ways. Small waves that had previously been unable to make it upstream against the river flow now wended their way inland. The early flooding tide had

10. A small tidal bore on the River Taf, Carmarthenshire.

produced a small change in the nature of the water surface, but not the bore I had come to see.

I got into the car and drove inland to a place where it was possible to park and then follow a short section of the Welsh coast path down to the river bank. The place wasn't perfect: a bend in the river obscured my view of any approaching bore, but I could find no better site. I was looking in the wrong direction when I heard the bore arriving – not a roar so much as the gentler gurgling sound of water in a hurry. The bore appeared, coming around the bend intact, a short set of waves probably no more than 10cm high, which then split around a shingle bank in the middle of the river. The two parts of the bore merged again on the other side of the bank, creating a pattern of criss-crossing waves. The bank was covered in seconds and the bore proceeded quickly upstream as a series of waves. The time was 5pm. The turn of the tide had travelled from Laugharne to my observation site – a distance of 4.5km – in a little under an hour. Somewhere on its way it had formed itself into a small, perfectly formed bore. It was only a tiny disturbance of the water surface, limping its way inland, but it was exhilarating to see it. It lifted my spirits for days afterwards.

Large tidal bores – those on the Trent and Severn, for example – appear as though nothing can stop them. The bore on the Taf looked as though anything would stop it. Several times, during the minute or two I watched it, the bore seemed to run out of steam, lose its identity and then re-form. It was teetering right on the edge of existence. It's far from the greatest bore in the world but, because of its very fragile nature, it might be a good one to study the processes necessary for bore formation.

The tidal limit

The furthest point inland that feels the effect of the tide is known as the tidal limit. This marks the landward extent of tidal influence, where the tide wave runs out of energy or reaches a point higher than the high tide at the estuary mouth. The tidal limit on an 'ordinary tide' (that is, half way between neaps and springs) is marked on Ordnance Survey Landranger maps (but not, for some reason, on the larger-scale Explorer maps). The distance

Table 1

Estuary	Tidal range at mouth (m) on an average tide	Width at mouth (km)	Estimated high tide depth at mouth (m)	Distance to tidal limit (km) *=weir	Distance over which width reduced by one-half (km)
Dee	5.4	8.4	10 3	33.5*	6.9
Clwyd	5.3	0.1	8	6.5	1.8
Conwy	5.0	0.2	13	21.5	4.1
Dwyryd	3.4	1.2	5.1	13.5	1.6
Mawddach	3.8	0.25	19	12	1.6
Dyfi	3.0	1.0	4	15	1.4
Teifi	2.8	1.75	2.7	9	1.6
Cleddau	4.2	2.5	20	34.2*	6.9
Taf	4.4	1.5	5	12.5	1.6
Towy	4.4	3.5	5	12.5	1.6
Loughor	5.2	3.5	7	20	3.0
Usk	8.4	0.6	14	24	3.6
Wye	9.0	0.75	11.3	24.5	5.8

of the tidal limit (taken from these maps) from the mouth of the major Welsh estuaries is listed in the table above. In some cases, the tidal limit is a man-made weir: we can take it that the tide would reach further inland if this artificial limit didn't exist. Tidal influence is felt furthest inland on the Cleddau estuary – both the eastern and western branches – in Pembrokeshire and on the river Dee in north-east Wales. The tidal range at the mouth of the Cleddau is not particularly great, but Pembrokeshire is a relatively flat county and the tidal wave is able to travel inland unimpeded by a steeply rising landscape. The same is true of the Dee advancing into the Cheshire countryside. Elsewhere, because of the steeply rising

hinterland, tides in Wales don't make it very far inland compared to other parts of the world. The tides on the Amazon, for example, can be detected 1000km from the sea.

The tidal range at the tidal limit is generally small – just a few centimetres – and it would take a careful and patient observer to measure it. It is interesting, nevertheless, because the water that rises and falls at this limit is fresh, rather than salty. Salt water from the sea doesn't usually make it up to the tidal limit. Instead, the high tide in the estuary acts as a dam which holds the river water back. It is the backing up of fresh water at the time of high tide in the estuary that raises the water level at the tidal limit. Between the highest reach of the salt water tide and the tidal limit, there is a stretch of river which shallows and deepens with tidal frequency but is never salty: a unique ecological environment.

11. *The inland limit of the tide. County Hall on the western Cleddau river in Pembrokeshire, where the tide is felt 34.2km inland;* 12. *The tidal limit on the Mawddach at the old bridge in Dolgellau, 12km from the mouth.*

The shape of estuaries

If I were asked to sketch a map of an estuary, it would be widest at the mouth (although in reality there is often a 'narrows' directly at the mouth, a spit of sand created by wave action and currents directed along the shore). My sketch of an estuary would then have a tapered width, narrowing up to the tidal limit, where it becomes a river. Many real estuaries do indeed have a shape something like this and the width of the estuary decreases with distance inland in a special way. The change in width in moving a set distance – say a kilometre – inland is a fixed fraction of the width at the start of the move.

For example, imagine an estuary that is 10km wide at the mouth narrows by 10% with each kilometre travelled inland. Then 1 km from the mouth, the width will be 9km (90% of 10km), 2 km inland it will be 8.9km (90% of 9km), 3km inland 8km (90% of 8.9km) and so on. The change in width is a fixed fraction of the original width, but the numerical value of the change decreases with each kilometre inland. This gives the estuary its characteristic fluted, or trumpet, shape on a map. Mathematicians call this rate of change in width an *exponential decay*. Not all estuaries have this shape exactly along their whole length but it is surprising how well an exponential decay in width fits the shape of many estuaries (as long as they are not confined to man-made channels), at least for part of their length.

With an exponential decay, the width keeps getting less as you travel inland without actually ever reaching zero. It's analogous to the decay of radioactive material, whose mass also decays exponentially with time. We can borrow a concept from radioactivity and apply it to estuary shapes. The half life of a radioactive isotope is the time taken for the mass to decay to half its initial value. We can define the *half length* of an estuary as the distance over which the width shrinks to half its initial value. The half length can be determined by measuring widths on an Ordnance Survey map. I have done this, using the widths at high tide and fitting a curve to them. The resulting half lengths are shown in the table above. There is a reasonably good relationship between the half-length and the tidal limit.

It is a curious thing to find natural features which have a shape that appears

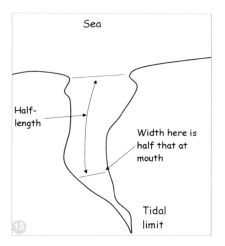

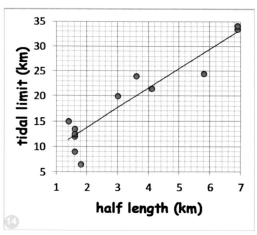

to follow a mathematical law. Snowflakes have a six-fold radial symmetry and snail shells have a shape called a logarithmic spiral. Why should estuaries take a form in which the width decreases with distance inland in a particular way? It has been suggested that this is the natural shape of a channel created by the tide acting on erodible material (such as the sand and mud). Crucially, it is a feature of estuaries with an exponential shape that the peak speed of the flood tidal current is *the same* along the length of the estuary. This is so because the current is set by the volume of water that flows through any cross-section of the estuary in a given time divided by the area of the section. At the mouth of the estuary there is a large volume flow on the flood tide (the tidal prism) but this is divided by a large cross-sectional area. Moving inland in an exponential estuary, the tidal prism reduces but the cross sectional area reduces in proportion. For an exponentially-shaped estuary, the

13. *Sketch of the shape of an estuary;*
14. *The relationship between the tidal limit and the estuary half-length.*

maximum value of the flood current is constant at all points.

It is possible that estuaries have adjusted their shape to preserve this constancy, with position, of the flood current. Currents erode sediments, carry them around and deposit them. There may be a critical current speed at which a section of an estuary comes into equilibrium. Currents faster than the critical speed will erode sediment and slower currents will leave sediment behind. At the critical speed, the rate at which sediment is eroded is exactly balanced by the rate at which it is deposited (this idea is called the *critical velocity hypothesis* and is well described by the American oceanographer Carl Friedrichs). According to this hypothesis, if a section of estuary is wider than predicted by the exponential rule, the flow is slower than the critical velocity. Sediment is deposited at that point, making the section narrower until the flow increases to the critical velocity. Conversely, if a section of estuary is too narrow, the current erodes the bank, increasing the cross-section to the point where the current falls to the critical velocity. It's a neat idea and the critical velocity that comes from fitting theoretical shapes to real estuaries works out at about 1 m/s, which is close to the maximum flood speed seen in many estuaries. If the hypothesis is correct it means that estuaries have adjusted their shape over hundreds of years to reach a state of equilibrium. This is an important point to be remembered by planners who propose to change the shape of an estuary to reclaim land or dredge channels.

Salt Intrusion

The flood tide brings salt water from the sea into an estuary. Farmers who extract water from rivers for irrigation need to know if the river water is likely to be contaminated by salt and so have to be aware of tidal changes. As sea level rises, it is likely that salt will intrude further inland than it does at present.

Sea water is denser than fresh water because of the salt it contains. One cubic metre of seawater weighs about 1025kg compared to 1000kg for the same volume

15. *The Seiont estuary, Caernarfon, at high and 16. at low tide.*

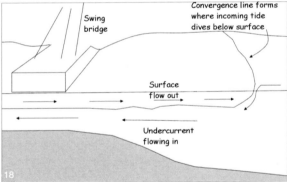

of freshwater. The difference is not great, but it is enough to affect the way that the tide gets into some estuaries. One way that this can happen is that the denser salt water coming in with the tide flows *under* the less dense river water already in the estuary at low water. This is not common in Welsh estuaries, but it can happen, especially in winter when there is a lot of river water and at places (and on days) where the tide is small.

The Seiont estuary at Caernarfon in north Wales is a small estuary nestling up to the medieval castle at the south-west end of the Menai Strait. It is a popular spot for small boats and a tourist magnet in the summer. At the mouth of the estuary there is a swing bridge which can be opened to let larger boats enter and leave the harbour.

Because of its small size, the volume of water that flows in and out of the Seiont with the tide is not great and the currents are relatively gentle. One damp morning in February I stood on the swing bridge and watched the tide come

17. The swing bridge at the mouth of the Seiont River; 18. Sketch of how the tide enters the Seiont as an undercurrent; 19. The convergence line, beyond the swans and marked by the red arrow, is at the edge of the plume front at the mouth of the Seiont.

in. At the start of the morning, the boats in the harbour were lying on their side in the mud. By lunchtime, they were bobbing on the high tide. The tide had certainly come in but, all morning the water appeared to have been flowing gently under the swing bridge *out of the harbour*. What must have been happening, although I couldn't see it, was that water was flowing into the harbour along the bottom, beneath the river water flowing out to sea at the surface. Each second, the inflow was bringing a little more water into the estuary than was removed by the surface outflow and so there was a net transport of water inwards. This kind of flow, with currents travelling in different directions at different depths, is called *sheared* flow. Richard Nunes-Vaz, who has dived into these murky waters, reports that you can see the underwater flows travelling in opposite directions and that waves form on the interface between the salt and fresh water.

The fresh water flowing out of the Seiont, even on a flood tide, spreads out over the surface of the Menai Strait, forming something

known as a *river plume*. At the edge of the plume, freshwater flowing outwards meets salt water flowing into the harbour. The two flows converge on the edge of the plume and the salt water dives under the plume here. Any floating material carried by either flow collects at this point, and marks the edge of the plume. In general, lines of flotsam in the sea mark places where currents are converging and water is forced downwards, leaving buoyant material at the surface. As the tide rises in the Menai Strait, the Seiont's river plume is pushed back towards the swing bridge

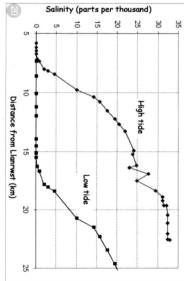

20. *Longitudinal variation of salinity in the Conwy estuary at high and low tide.*

and, sometimes, it is forced right under the bridge and into the harbour making something called a *tidal intrusion front*. The favoured conditions for this to happen are large tides in summer when the river flow is small.

The Seiont is unusual amongst Welsh estuaries for exhibiting this sheared flow.

21. Sully Island, near Penarth is a tidal island accessible by causeway at low tide;
22. Visitors are advised to check tide times before making the crossing.

In other estuaries, with a larger tidal prism, the turbulence generated by the incoming tide mixes the salt and fresh water and the mixture travels upstream. The mixture contains more salt near the mouth of the estuary and less salt further inland and so a gradient of salt content is created.

The salt content of water is called *salinity* and is usually expressed as parts of salt per thousand parts of water. Typical salinity in the offshore waters around Wales is between 30 and 34 parts per thousand and the salinity of fresh water is zero (water tastes brackish to our tongues at salinities above 0.5 parts per thousand).

Salinity can be measured with instruments (the most common way is through the change it makes in the electrical conductivity of the water) and, by racing up an estuary in a speed boat fitted with such an instrument, it is possible to measure the gradient of salinity. A fast survey like this can only measure the salinity at the surface, but in an estuary with large tides there will be little difference in saltiness between the surface and the bottom. The dense waters with high salinity near the mouth of the estuary try to flow under the less dense waters inland but they are quickly mixed by the tides.

The whole pattern of the longitudinal salinity variation in the estuary is pushed in and out of the estuary by the tide, so that at any place the water is saltiest at high tide. Animals and plants living in the estuary have to cope with the large changes in salinity. Some creatures have adapted to it and thrive under these conditions but others find the change in the salinity of the ambient water a difficult thing to cope with. The extent of the change depends on how far the tide moves a parcel of water in and out of the estuary: the distance a piece of water moves between low and high tide is called the *tidal displacement*. As a rule of thumb, the tidal displacement in kilometres is 14 times the maximum current speed in metres per second. In an estuary in which the maximum current is 1.5m/s, a parcel of water will move back and forth about 21 km with each tide.

An island in a tidal stream in an estuary will be bathed in different salinities as the tide ebbs and flows and can make a home to adaptable marine and freshwater creatures. In her book 'Memories of Welsh

Islands' the naturalist Mary Gillham describes the barnacles on Sully Island in the Bristol Channel.

Here you can find two types of barnacle which are rarely found together. The sea-living Balanus Cretanus goes no

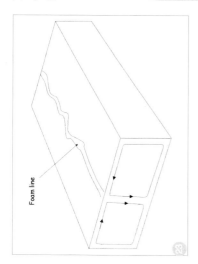

23. Surface foam lines indicate converging currents which sink at the foam line leaving buoyant material behind; 24. Axial convergence along the Conwy estuary on a flood tide, viewed from the castle; 25. and 26. A small boat moored in the river follows the meanders of the axial convergence.

Foam line

further up and the estuarine Balanus Improvisus goes no further down. This last penetrates right up almost to the bridge at Gloucester, where brave hearts riding the Severn bore finally fall off their surf boards.

More about foam lines

Foam lines, sometimes stretching as far as the eye can see, are frequent features of the surface of the sea. On a windy day, for example, you may see a series of parallel foam lines, called wind rows, stretching along in the direction the wind is blowing. Surface currents converge from both sides of the foam line and, since the water has nowhere else to go, it dives down, leaving any floating detritus behind at the surface.

A foam line which puts in a regular repeat appearance along the central axis of the Conwy estuary was first noticed by John Simpson of Bangor University. The incoming tide carries salt water upstream most quickly at the surface and in the centre of the estuary, where it is least affected by the friction of the channel bed and sides. The water along this central surface axis is denser than the water below. The dense water sinks to be replaced by water flowing in from the sides of the estuary. The flows from the side create an *axial convergence line*, marked by foam. On the Conwy, the axial convergence appears as a foam line running up the estuary as far as the eye can see on a flood tide.

The flooding tide swirls from side to side as it moves up the estuary and this eddying movement is faithfully followed by the foam line, which picks out the local current direction. Small boats moored along the axial convergence sway from side to side as the eddies pass. This complicated motion is part of the turbulence in the estuary: small whirlpools superimposed on the main flow. The turbulence is usually invisible but, in this case, the foam line and the occasional boat moored in just the right place allow us to see it in action.

A balancing act

The flood tide brings salt water into an estuary, where it mixes with the water

Welsh estuaries contain several hundred times more water – and salt – at high tide than they do at low tide. This is the estuary of the river Wye at Chepstow photographed on a low (27) and a high water (28).

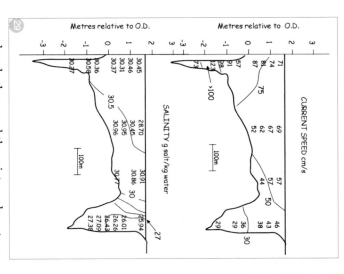

29. *A cross-section of the Conwy estuary during the flood tide showing the current speed (top) and salinity (bottom).*

low tide, the volume of water in an estuary 20km long, 10m wide and 2m deep is 0.4 million m³. The same length of estuary at high tide might be 500m wide and 10m deep and contain 100 million m³ of water. The volume of water in Welsh estuaries increases and decreases by a factor of several hundred every tide.

In the long term, the water that flows into the estuary through tides and river flows must exactly balance the water that flows out again (apart from any evaporation from the surface). This requirement is called the *water balance*. There may not be a water balance over a single tidal cycle: the estuary may be a little fuller or emptier at the end of a single tide than at the start, but that is not sustainable for long. Averaged over a long enough time, the water going in must equal that going out. Similarly, there must be a *salt balance*. The mass of salt brought into the estuary by a succession of flood tides must be balanced by the mass of salt removed by the ebb tides over the same period. If that is not the case the estuary will gradually get more, or less, saline with time.

Experimentalists like to check that already there and the mixture departs on the next ebb tide. The change to the appearance of the estuary as this process happens twice a day is a dramatic one. At what 'must be' can be confirmed by observation. Testing the idea of a salt balance requires careful measurements of currents, depths, widths and salinities at time intervals over a tidal cycle, or longer, to determine the mass of salt entering and leaving the estuary. This is labour-intensive (but mostly fun) team-work involving small boats and profiling with instruments at different spots across a section of the estuary. Surveys like this reveal variations in the speed of the flow and the salinity that could not be guessed at. For example, the flood tide might favour one bank over the other. In this case, the flow will be faster (and the water saltier) on this bank during the flood. The data can be used to calculate the salt flux (the mass of salt crossing the observation section per unit time) and, by adding up values of the salt flux over a tidal cycle, the net mass of salt entering or leaving the estuary can be determined.

The results of a number of experimental campaigns tell us that Welsh estuaries do not normally balance their salt budget over a single tidal cycle. They are in a constant balancing act. There is a natural, or equilibrium, volume of water

and mass of salt that an estuary should hold and it is constantly seeking to adjust to reach this equilibrium. In this sense, estuaries are in a similar situation to a tight-rope walker traversing Niagara falls. The walker is trying to keep in balance and leans to one side and then the other to counteract the effect of buffeting wind gusts. The 'buffets' that affect the salt balance of an estuary are changes in tidal range and river flow. Some years ago, the tacit assumption was that estuaries were close to equilibrium most of the time and only occasionally pushed out of balance by, for example, a rapid increase in river flow. The experimental evidence now suggests that, in fact, estuaries are rarely in equilibrium. Most of the time, they are importing or exporting salt and water in an attempt to reach their equilibrium state. A good question that we don't really know the answer to is how long does it take an estuary to settle down after being pushed out of balance?

5. Tides in the history – and future – of Wales

The Roman legions arriving in Wales in the 1st century AD faced a loose alliance of Celtic tribes ready to fight. They also faced the Welsh tides. The large tides of the Welsh coast, particularly on the Bristol Channel must have seemed astonishing to people from southern Europe where, by that time they were already a valuable commodity and so had probably been around for a while. Then, and now, boats could enter and leave Mediterranean harbours whenever they liked. In contrast, small Welsh harbours dry out at low tide and are metres-deep six hours later. Tying your boat up to a harbour wall in these circumstances involves a complex arrangement of ropes. Living in a land of tides presents problems, but it also provides opportunities. Tides have an energy which is virtually limitless and is also (unusually for green energy sources) very predictable. There is growing interest in seeing if we can extract some of that energy and convert it into useful electricity. The idea of getting the tide to do work for you is not a new one in Wales, though. There is history here.

Medieval Fish Traps

It is difficult to be sure when fish traps first appeared in the country. There is written evidence that traps in the seaside village of Aberarth in Ceredigion were offered to the monastery of Strata Florida in 1184. At that time they were already a valuable commodity and so had probably been around for a while. A fish trap is a barrier in a tidal estuary or harbour (or just on a beach) which allowed the water to escape as the tide ebbed but kept the fish back. The Welsh were prolific builders of fish traps: there are the remains of dozens of them to be seen around the coast (they seemed to share this fascination with the Maori inhabitants of New Zealand, another country with a history of trapping fish). Some traps, once visible on the beach, have disappeared in recent years, probably covered by sand. An example is the fish trap at Tenby, shown on a 19th century map but not visible today.

The fish-trap industry in Wales declined in the 19th century and had

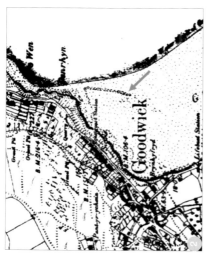

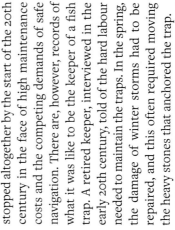

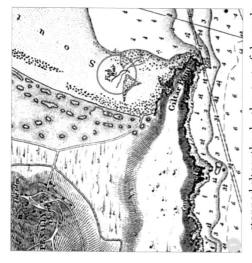

stopped altogether by the start of the 20th century in the face of high maintenance costs and the competing demands of safe navigation. There are, however, records of what it was like to be the keeper of a fish trap. A retired keeper, interviewed in the early 20th century, told of the hard labour needed to maintain the traps. In the spring, the damage of winter storms had to be repaired, and this often required moving the heavy stones that anchored the trap.

Different styles of trap were favoured in different parts of the country. A common design took the form of a V-shape pointing seaward. The base of the trap was constructed of stones to provide a strong foundation and on top of this there would be a fence made of plaited tree branches. In some of the best maintained traps, the wooden poles that held the fence survive, although more commonly it is just the foundation stones that have lasted. As the tide ebbed, fish

would have been caught in the trap and could be collected at low water.

The remains of a V-shaped trap can be seen at Goodwick beach in Pembrokeshire. The full V-shape is marked on the early maritime charts of Lewis Morris dating from 1748, but the trap was partly destroyed during the construction of the railway lines into Goodwick in the early 20th century. What's left is a line of stones clearly visible at low tide. Another example can be seen at Lligwy beach on Anglesey. This one is crescent-shaped and 140 paces long. It is a humbling experience to see it close up; the stones are large and heavy and would have been dragged into place by muscle power alone.

The two main Welsh words for a fish trap are Argae and Cored and evidence for the existence of fish traps remains in place names. The fish trap on the River Teifi, Cored Cilgerran, is described by Gerald of Wales. Ynys Gorad Goch, an island in the Menai Strait was owned in the 16th century by the diocese of Bangor and the rent included a barrel of herrings caught in the fish traps on the island.

Tide Mills

Bread made from wheat flour has been part of the diet of many civilisations since prehistoric times. To make flour, wheat has to be ground to a fine powder. This can be done in small quantities by hand, but to make enough flour to feed a village, some kind of milling process is needed. In pre-industrial days, the wheat was ground between two circular mill stones, one laid on top of the other like two biscuits in a packet. The lower stone was laid flat on the floor of the mill and the upper, runner stone, turned on top of this, grinding grains of wheat into flour.

To be effective, the stones had to be heavy. Mill stones weigh about a ton each and it takes a lot of energy to make the runner stone turn on top of its mate. Before the industrial revolution, this energy was supplied by natural processes: wind and running water. Wind-powered mills were popular on Anglesey, the bread-basket of Wales, where wheat was grown and the wind blows across the gentle hills of the island. Anglesey had more windmills than any other county. In the more hilly parts of the country, water mills were more practical. Water is heavy and even a

3. Medieval fish traps at Goodwick in Pembrokeshire and 4. Lligwy on Anglesey.

small stream could fill buckets on a water wheel and drive a mill.

At a few coastal locations, mills were constructed to harness the energy in the tide. Tide mills are relatively rare. There are five restored mills in the UK, one of which is in Wales, at Carew in Pembrokeshire. Here, the mill is located on a causeway damming the Carew River. When the tide is rising, water is allowed to flow freely through flood gates into the upper part of the river creating a Mill Pond. At high tide, the flood gates can be closed and the Mill Pond drained through sluices under the mill, driving two water wheels.

Seeing a tide mill close up leaves a strong impression of the power available in dammed-up water, even when the drop in level is just a few metres. The water from the mill pond at Carew cascades down through gaps in the top of the causeway. Sitting on top of one of these cascades, one can sense the force that nature (and man) has created. It is a shame that there aren't more working examples of these quietly powerful structures.

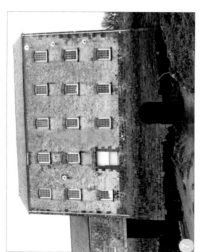

5. Carew Tide Mill. Water impounded in the mill pond to the left of the causeway;
6. A tidal waterfall in the causeway;
7. The Mill viewed from downstream. The water wheels are located in the two doorways (one arched, one flat-topped);
8. A mill wheel.

Storm surges

Tides are not the only cause of high water levels at the coast. An onshore wind coupled with locally low atmospheric pressure can produce elevated coastal sea levels called a *storm surge*. Negative storm surges, in which sea level is depressed at the coast, also happen but these are not normally a cause for concern, unless you are on a large ship manoeuvring in shallow water at the time. Positive storm surges coupled with a high water on a spring tide and ferocious storm waves can lift sea water over the top of coastal flood defences and create havoc.

Wales, along with all maritime nations, is vulnerable to flooding by the sea. A severe storm breached the sea defences at Towyn in North Wales in 1990. Thousands of homes were damaged and many people were evacuated, although no lives were lost as a direct result of the flooding. In the winter of 2019/2020, storms (which now had names like Ciara and Dennis) forced the closure of the Cambrian coast railway, partly because of landslides but also because of breaches of the sea defences.

The south Wales coast around Newport in Gwent is particularly vulnerable to storm surges. This is partly because of the converging shape of the Bristol Channel and the fact that it faces south-west into the prevailing winds, but also because the land here – the Gwent levels – is low-lying and flat. The levels, intersected with drainage channels and protected by a high wall look and feel more like the Netherlands than Wales. Even some of the village names – Wentlooge, for example – sound Dutch.

The greatest loss of life from a sudden natural disaster in the UK in the past 500 years happened here in the winter of 1607. Between 500 and 2000 people living in small villages and remote farms were killed in floods in the Monmouthshire and Somerset levels on either side of the Bristol Channel. Contemporary accounts, with some adjustment to spelling, could well be used in modern news bulletins:

Let us fix our eyes upon theise late swellings of the outrageous waters, which of late now hapnd in diverse partes of the Realme, together with the

overflowing of the Seas in divers and sundry places thereof: whole fruitful valleys, being now overwhelmed and drowned with these most unfortunate and unseasonable salt waters. Many men that were rich in the morning when they rose out of their beds, were made poore before noone the same day.

* * *

There is some question about the exact cause of the flooding. A suggestion a few years ago was that this was the work of a tsunami created by an underwater earthquake, but the timing of the flood coinciding with a high water on a spring tide, contemporary weather records and the absence of earthquakes at the time, make a storm surge a more likely culprit.

The great flood of 1607 is commemorated by plaques on a number of local churches, with marks made at the time of the flood showing the height that the sea reached. They take some finding, though. My wife and I walked around St Bridget's three times looking for a sign. 'Perhaps it's in this bit here', said Faith, pointing to a

9. St Thomas Church, Redwick recording the 1607 flood level. The word 'FLOOD' chiselled into the stone is about 5 feet above ground.

modern extension to the church building. I rang the vicar whose number was conveniently on the church notice board. He was a lovely chap, very helpful, but he didn't know anything about flood signs. 'Which church are you at?' he asked. 'I have several'.

At St. Mary the Virgin in Nash, there is a modern metal plaque on the north-east corner, furthest from the sea. The flood level mark is at shoulder height, about 5 feet from the ground. At St. Thomas's, Redwick the sign is an old one on the south-east corner, closest to the sea. The mark here is chiselled into a stone on the church wall, the single word 'FLOOD' with a brass or bronze bolt hammered into the wall just below shoulder height.

Scientific advances

The large tides and fast streams of Wales have attracted the attention of some of the greatest scientific minds. In the early 20th century, Sir Geoffrey Ingram Taylor (professor of Physics at Trinity College, Cambridge) worked out the effect of friction on the tide in the Irish Sea. Tidal streams, rubbing against the sea bed, lose energy through friction. This loss of energy is ultimately extracted from the earth's spin and the earth is very gradually slowing, and the day becoming longer, as a result. When Taylor first thought about this problem there was no established way for calculating frictional energy loss and so he had to develop his own methods: he found two ways to do this. The first was to use a rule established from studies of the wind blowing over the ground, that the friction force between a moving fluid and a solid surface depends on the square of the flow speed. The rate at which energy is lost from the flow then goes as the friction force multiplied by the flow speed and so depends on the cube of the flow speed. It was immediately obvious to Taylor that the tide would lose energy most rapidly at places with fast currents. The Irish Sea, with currents typically 1 m/s would use up energy 1,000,000 times faster than an Irish Sea-sized piece of the Atlantic Ocean, where the tidal currents are typically 1 cm/s. Taylor used observations at *tidal diamonds* (places where the Admiralty had measured currents) to calculate energy losses in the Irish Sea and he compared these to results from a second method based on the energy in the tide wave.

We saw in chapter 2 that the tide arrives at the Welsh coast as a wave which has travelled from the Atlantic south of Ireland. There is a second wave that enters the Irish Sea through the channel between northern Ireland and Scotland. Waves carry *energy*, potential energy in the height of the crest and kinetic energy in the currents beneath the surface. Taylor worked out how much energy was carried into the Irish Sea by these waves. He considered the energy in the waves that were coming into the Irish Sea and the smaller amount of energy in the waves that were reflected out again. The difference between the incoming and reflected energy, the net energy flux, must be used up by friction within the Irish Sea. This figure agreed with his calculations using the flow speeds. It was a brilliant piece of scientific work.

Taylor calculated that the Irish Sea, despite its small size, accounted for between 1 and 2% of global energy losses through tidal friction. His methods have since been applied to shallow seas with important tides all around the world. An extension of the method has been used in the deep ocean (a place which had

previously been thought not to be so important for tidal friction). This has led to the discovery that the deep ocean tide *does* lose energy, not through friction between currents and the bottom, but through the creation of waves called *internal tides* in the interior of the ocean.

Other discoveries about the tide, first made in Welsh waters are universally important and we have described some of these already in this book. They are mostly to do with the way that tides mix seawater, creating fronts and pushing salt water into estuaries. The Eagle Tower of Caernarfon Castle, for example, is known internationally by tidal scientists (who know nothing about Edward I) as the place that tidal intrusion fronts were first observed.

Tides and the weather

One aspect of the tide that hasn't received as much attention as it probably deserves is the effect it can have on the weather of coastal communities. Water has a high thermal capacity – it is much better at storing heat than the land. This is why coastal countries such as Wales have mild winters compared to a land locked country such as, to pick one at random – Czechoslavakia. The sea stores up heat in the summer and releases it in the winter, moderating the climate.

We can imagine that a similar thing could happen, in a more muted way, over a 24 hour period and that now the tide could play a role. On a cold winter's night, people living alongside a tidal river should feel milder conditions if the tide is in. The close proximity of a large body of relatively warm water would be expected to raise the air temperature by a degree or two and possibly prevent a frost. Conversely, on a hot summer's day the high tide will keep the air temperature down a bit compared to another hot day when the tide is out. These subtle changes of air temperature with the tide, if they actually happen, could also influence atmospheric pressure and humidity and so might affect other aspects of the weather such as wind and rain.

A number of people I have spoken to about this tell me that they believe there is a link between the weather and the tide. Someone who liked night fishing on the shore of the Menai Strait said that he looked forward to the wind dropping as the tide came in. I have heard that wind surfers on the river Dee in north Wales are convinced that wind conditions change as high water approaches. All this is anecdotal evidence, of course, but there are some hard observations to support the idea.

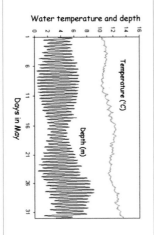

10. *Variations in the tide (blue) and water temperature (red) at Ynys Faelog in the Menai Strait in winter (left) and summer in the (right).*

Records of water temperature and depth near Ynys Faelog in the Menai Strait show that the temperature varies with the springs-neaps tidal cycle. The sense is different in winter and summer. In January, the waters of the strait are warmer (by a couple of degrees) on a spring tide. In May, the water is warmest on a neap tide. In both months, the variation with the springs-neaps tidal cycle is greater than the daily fluctuations of temperature.

11. Ynys Faelog is the island in the lower centre of the picture, joined to the main island of Anglesey by a causeway with a right-angled bend (photo: David Roberts).

We can think of ways that the tide might control the temperature of the water in the strait. In winter, offshore waters are warmer than shallow waters near the coast (this happens because they are deeper and better able to retain their summer heat). The tide brings offshore water into the strait and mixes it with the water already there. The reach of the tide and the strength of the mixing is greater at springs and so that's a possible explanation of why the water in the strait, in winter, is warmer on a spring tide. In summer, offshore waters will be cooler than the water in the strait and we would expect the effect to be reversed. The full process may not be as simple as I have just described but, whatever the reason, the temperature of the water in the Menai Strait varies with the fortnightly springs-neaps tidal cycle. It wouldn't be surprising if the temperature of the air above the strait and other aspects of the weather followed suit.

Electricity from the tide

As the world looks to find sustainable energy supplies, attention is turning to ways of extracting energy from the tide to

make electricity. Tides have two kinds of energy: kinetic energy in the horizontal flows and potential energy that is created every time the tide rises vertically. Welsh tides have plenty of both: the Welsh coast experiences some of the highest tides in the world as well as some spectacularly fast tidal currents. We are so well placed to take some of our energy from the tide that future generations will wonder what took us so long.

The simplest way to harness tidal power is to place a turbine in the way of a fast current: the marine equivalent of a windmill. A solid object placed in a flow of water feels a force as the water pushes against it. You can feel this force when you hold a knife blade under the tap. If the blade is horizontal, the force acts downwards, but if you turn the blade at an angle to the flow you can feel a sideways force as the water bounces off the knife. It is this sideways force, acting on an angled blade, that makes the turbine turn. The force is equal to the rate of change of water momentum as the water is deflected off the blade. Water momentum is proportional to the speed of flow and the rate at which the momentum changes also depends on the speed, and so the force the water exerts on the blade increases as the square of the flow speed.

In a turbine in the sea, the blades will spin up to a speed at which the turning force exerted by the current is matched by the drag force on the blade as it moves through the water. In a well-designed turbine the average speed of the moving blade will be close to the current speed. If a load is now placed on the turbine, by attaching it to a dynamo, the rotation speed will slow. The power output is then equal to the applied load multiplied by the turning speed of the rotor blades. Engineers can select the appropriate load to get the most electricity: too much load and the turbine will turn too slowly, too little and the turbine will turn quickly but not generate electricity as efficiently as it can.

Water is about a thousand times denser than air and so the change in momentum as the water bounces off a blade is much greater than that of air moving at the same speed. A water flow of 2 metres per second generates the same force as a wind speed of about 60 metres per second. The power output from a turbine depends on the force on the blade times the turning speed and increases as the cube of the flow speed. A tidal flow of 2 metres per second has eight times the power of a 1 m.s^{-1} flow. It is therefore important to find places with fast currents to generate the most electricity. The prime sites for tidal turbines on the Welsh coast are in the sounds between islands and the mainland, in the Bristol Channel and off the north coast of Anglesey. A big attraction of electricity generated

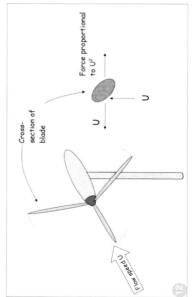

12. *As flowing water hits the blades of a tidal turbine, it generates a turning force proportional to the square of the flow speed.*

in this way is that it is reliable: tidal streams are very predictable and a number of turbines can be sited at places with different phases of the tide so that electricity can be generated continuously.

Tidal turbines have their problems. Water can flow around the turbine rather than through the blades and so the turbine is not particularly efficient at extracting the energy in the flow. Sea water is a corrosive fluid and maintaining a moving

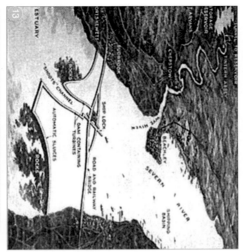

13. *A tidal power scheme for the Severn estuary as it appeared in Popular Mechanics in 1921.*

structure in the sea and getting the electricity it generates safely to shore presents a severe challenge to today's technology. A trial of a turbine in Ramsey Sound was abandoned after a short while because of mechanical failure. There are plans to try clever designs to extract more energy from the flow. In one of these, the dynamo is fitted to an underwater kite tethered to the sea bed. The kite will soar through the flow at high speed and generate more electricity than a fixed turbine.

Some of the problems with turbines sited in the open sea can be overcome by constructing a tidal barrage or dam wall. The idea here is the same as that used at the Carew tidal mill. A portion of sea is enclosed by a wall. Water is allowed to flow freely into the enclosure as the tide rises and then is made to flow out through a tight passage through electricity-generating turbines as the tide falls. A structure such as this is harnessing the potential energy in the tide: the energy created as the sea is lifted in the earth's gravity. The potential energy is proportional to the mass of water times the vertical distance it is lifted. Both these quantities depend on the tidal range and so the power output from a barrage increases as the *square* of the tidal range.

Barrages are therefore best placed in places with the biggest tidal range. It also helps to use the local geography and so bays, or estuaries, with a large tidal range are the favoured places. In Wales, barrages enclosing tidal lagoons have been proposed for Swansea, Cardiff and Newport in the south and Colwyn Bay in the north. The most ambitious project would be to place a barrage across a part of the Severn estuary. Plans for harnessing the biggest tides in the country have been around for a long time, one scheme being discussed in the magazine Popular Mechanics in 1921. The Severn tidal barrage is a high-cost, high-reward project. It would be one of the biggest engineering undertakings in the world and it could generate up to 5% of the UK's electricity and help the country meet its renewable energy targets.

There are environmental consequences to any tidal barrage scheme. The water enters the enclosed lagoon more quickly than it can escape and as a result, sea level is pumped up within the lagoon. There is, more or less, a permanent high tide inside (although proponents of tidal lagoons say that this can be avoided with clever design). Sediments brought in by rivers are trapped within the lagoon, which will silt up and need dredging. The large tidal range and regular flushing that existed before the lagoon will disappear and there can be a build-up of pollution. An immediate impact is that the sand and mud-banks, formerly exposed at low tide and important feeding grounds for birds, will be lost. There is a point of view, however, that eliminating the tide and creating perpetual high water at the coast is preferable to seeing and smelling a great expanse of mud at low water. The Cardiff Bay barrage was built to impound the sea partly for these aesthetic reasons.

Changes in Sea Level

Sea level is steadily rising. We know this from the long records at tide gauges at important ports and, in recent years, from the evidence provided by radar altimeters on satellites orbiting the earth. Sea level around the British Isles has risen by about 15cm, or 6 inches, in the last century and it looks as though the rate of rise has accelerated in the last decade. The cause of this rise is generally agreed to be a mixture of thermal expansion of the ocean and added water from glaciers melting as the planet has warmed since the industrial revolution.

Coastal flood defences, already stretched by present sea levels, will be overcome more often in the future. In Wales, the village of Fairbourne near Barmouth faces an uncertain future. The village is a relatively modern one, built in the middle 1800's on a low-lying salt marsh. There is an impressive sea defence wall, built of stones and concrete blocks which is occasionally overtopped by storm waves and high tides. With rising sea level and no change to the defences, this will become a more frequent event. It is possible the village may have to be evacuated in the next few decades if sea level continues to rise at the current rate.

Unfortunately, it is no longer in our power to stop sea level rising further. Extra heat already added to the ocean surface will continue to be gradually mixed into the interior of the ocean over the next few decades. As the body of the ocean warms it will expand; this will happen even if

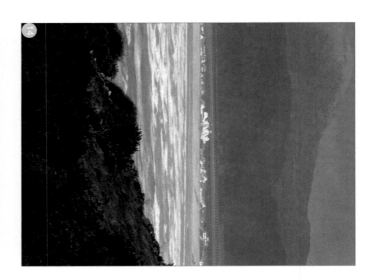

14. *Fairbourne, seen in a long distance shot from the south with Snowdonia towering behind. The sea defence wall 15, constructed of concrete and stones, may not be enough to protect the village from rising sea levels.*

The Tides of Wales

carbon dioxide emissions are stopped overnight. The exact increase in the height of the sea surface in the future depends on how emissions go and what happens to the water currently stored in glaciers. The UK Meteorological Office predicts a rise of up to 1.12 metres by 2100.

Superimposed on the rise in sea level are fluctuations in sea level associated with the weather and the seasons. Sea level at Menai Bridge, for example, can be 20 to 30 cm higher in winter than in summer. Seasonal changes in sea level such as this are common and are produced by low atmospheric pressure and strong offshore winds in winter piling the water up against the shore. A number of Welsh coastal communities are currently troubled by sea flooding on high spring tides. In some cases it is no more than a nuisance, but it could become more serious as sea level rises further. Planners at county and national level need to know how to prepare for the effects of rising sea level and to mitigate for it.

Lower Town in Fishguard is a picture-postcard fishing village, very popular with visitors in the summer. Tourists park in the town's car park and go for a walk along the sea front. Unfortunately, the car park is prone to flooding on high tides, even on calm days, and the unwary can be caught out. Experience suggests that the car park is flooded when the tide in the harbour is 5 metres above Lowest Astronomical Tide. That's equivalent to a tide at Milford Haven of 7.25 m above LAT. We saw in chapter 1 how the height of the high waters at Milford varied over the course of a year. The same data can be used to work out the number of days in a year that the high waters *exceed* a particular height. Using just one year's data we can see that the tide at Milford exceeds 7.25 m (and so we anticipate that the car park will

flood) on about 30 days in the year. How will this figure change as sea level rises? If the tides stay the same and sea level rose by half a metre then the floods will happen when the tide height exceeds 6.75 m (half a metre less than the current level). That will happen on about 90 days a year – 3 times more frequently than now. It would, of course, be better to use several years of data to do this analysis, but you can get the idea of how it would be done from the explanation above.

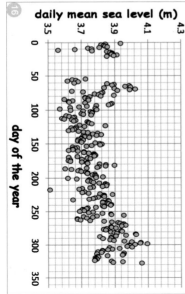

16. *Daily mean sea level in the Menai Strait in 2001; 17. and 18. Fishguard harbour at low and high tide.*

defences, for example. If mean sea level rises and the tidal range is *reduced*, what happens exactly, to the heights of the high waters?

We saw in chapter 2 that the tide travels around the coast of Wales as a wave. It bounces off coasts and the tide on the west and north coast of the country behaves as the sum of incoming and reflected waves. There is a place, currently around Aberdyfi, where the two waves are exactly out of phase: it is low water in one when it is high water in the other and vice versa. The two waves interfere destructively at this place and there is a minimum in tidal range.

The exact location of the place this happens is three lunar hours in (one-way) wave travel time from the reflecting coast at Liverpool. Tide waves travel at a speed which depends on the water depth. If the water gets deeper they will travel faster and the point of destructive interference and minimum tidal range will move further from Liverpool. Places south of Aberdyfi will then see a reduction in tidal range (and places immediately north will have bigger tides). This effect may help

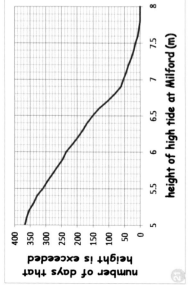

19. *Sign warning of flooding in Fishguard's lower town Car Park; 20. Fishguard Lower Town Car park near the top of the flood; 21. The number of days in a year that a given height of high tide at Milford is exceeded.*

Future tides

The Fishguard lower town case is a particular example of a local problem but it raises an important general question: will tides stay the same as sea level rises? Figures for sea level rise refer to the *mean* level but what is important in many cases is the *maximum* level: the mean level plus the height of the tide on top of that. It is the maximum level that matters to flood limit flooding at Fishguard, which lies south of Aberdyfi, although probably not much. A one-metre rise in sea level will move the point of minimum range just a few kilometres south.

Today, we are only marginally better at predicting the future than the Celts who faced the Roman legions two thousand years ago. We can anticipate that sea level will rise faster in coming decades and that coastal flooding will become more frequent. We can hope that clever engineers will develop methods of extracting a large part of our energy needs from the tide. One thing that we can be sure of is that the tides will not stop. They will continue to rise and fall, through political

upheaval and plague. Twice-daily tides will be made in the ocean as long as the earth spins beneath the moon. Gradually, very gradually, the earth's spin will slow because of friction on tidal flows and the planet will come to rest with the same hemisphere facing the moon. At that time, twice-daily tides will no longer pass over the face of the ocean, although there will still be tides of sorts. Monthly tides will be created by the variation in the earth-moon distance and yearly tides by the earth's movement about the sun. All this is very far into the future, though. Most estimates have it happening after the sun has run out of nuclear fuel and the solar system is lying in darkness.

Further Reading

Chapter 1 Raising tides

P. Caton *No boat required: Exploring Tidal Islands*. Matador, 2012

E. Naylor *Moonstruck: How Lunar Cycles affect Life*. Oxford University Press, 2015

A.H.W. Robinson *Lewis Morris – an early Welsh hydrographer*. The Journal of Navigation, 1958

P.L. Woodworth *Three Georges and one Richard Holden: The Liverpool tide table makers*. Transactions of the Historic Society of Lancashire and Cheshire, 2002

Chapter 2 Tidal Patterns

A.T. Doodson and H.D. Warburg *Admiralty Manual of Tides*. HMSO, 1941

D. Pugh and P.L. Woodworth *Sea Level Science*. Cambridge University Press, 2004

D.G. Bowers and E.M. Roberts *Tides: a Very Short Introduction*. Oxford University Press, 2019

M.Marten *Sea Change*. Kehrer Books, 2012

Chapter 3 Sea straits and sounds

R.M. Lockley *Letters from Skokholm*. Little Toller, 2010

R. Alexander *Waterfalls of Stars: Ten years on Skomer Island*. Seren Books, 2017

Chapter 4 Tides in Estuaries and Rivers

M.E. Gillham *Memories of Welsh Islands* Gwasg Dinefwr. Press, 2004

E. Gruffudd *The Conwy Estuary Explored*. Gwasg Carreg Gwalch, 2018

B. Waters *The Bristol Channel*. Dent, 1955

Chapter 5 Tides in the History – and Future – of Wales

D. Cartwright *Tides, a scientific history*. Cambridge University Press, 1999

F. Murphy, H. Wilson and M. Page *Medieval and early post-medieval fish traps: a threat related assessment 2012*. Dyfed Archaeological Trust, 2013

Risk Management Solutions *1607 Bristol Channel Floods: 400 Year Retrospective*. RMS Special Report, 2007

Glossary

Acceleration is the rate of change of velocity in a flow. Tidal flows accelerate as they speed up, slow down and change direction. They can also accelerate from one part of the flow to another. A force is needed to create acceleration and in most cases this is provided by a sloping sea surface making a pressure gradient force.

An axial convergence is a foam line down the central axis of an estuary formed by water converging on the line from both sides. The water sinks at the convergence leaving behind floating detritus which creates the foam.

A Boundary layer is the part of a flow which is slowed down by a boundary, for example the sea bed or a shoreline.

The Coriolis effect is the apparent deflection of moving objects on the surface of a rotating Earth. The deflection is only apparent to people moving with the earth (to an observer in space the moving object is seen to be travelling in a straight line). The Coriolis effect deflects things to the right in the northern hemisphere.

Datum A fixed level from which the tide can be measured. Mean Sea Level and Lowest Astronomical Tide are examples of data.

Diffusion is the spreading of a substance from a region of high concentration to one of low concentration. In a fluid such as seawater, diffusion is produced by turbulent eddies.

A floc is a loose collection of small particles bound together with natural glues in seawater. In tidal waters, the flocs change their size with the tide, breaking up in strong flows and re-forming in slow ones.

Friction is experienced when tidal currents flow over the sea bed or next to a coastline. The friction force increases as the square of the flow speed and slows the water immediately in contact with the land, which then slows the water next to that and so on, creating a boundary layer.

A hydraulic jump is a transition in the flow from a state of high speed and low water level to one of slower speed and higher water level. There is a reduction in kinetic energy and an increase in potential energy at the jump.

Intertidal zone The region between high and low tide, which forms a special ecological niche for creatures that are adapted to immersion in sea water and exposure in the air.

Isolated turbidity maximum A region of turbid water in strong tidal streams that is isolated from any obvious source of material to make the turbidity. The suspended particles inside the maximum are small and diffuse into the surrounding water, where they form into flocs which diffuse back into the maximum.

Lowest Astronomical Tide The lowest level that the tide can be expected to fall at a place. It is equivalent to **Chart Datum** from which the depths on Admiralty Charts are measured.

Plume front is the boundary between fresh and salt water created when a river spreads out over the sea.

Pressure gradient force is a horizontal force created by a sloping sea surface. The pressure is greater under the high part of

the slope and this creates a force acting on the water in the down-slope direction. In tidal flows, the pressure gradient force either accelerates the flow or is needed to overcome friction, or a mixture of the two.

Spring and neap tides. Spring tides are a time of maximum tidal range, happening twice a month shortly after the time of new and full moon. Neap tides occur half-way between springs and are days of smaller tidal range.

A tidal bore is a moving hydraulic jump. It is the leading edge of the tidal wave advancing up an estuary. They can be seen on several Welsh estuaries.

Tidal force The difference between the moon's gravity at a point on the surface of the Earth and its value at the centre of the earth is the moon's tidal force on our planet. There is an equivalent, but smaller, tidal force exerted on the surface of the earth by the Sun.

Tidal intrusion front is a sharp surface boundary between fresh and salt water within an estuary. It is created when the flood tide pushes a plume front into the estuary.

Tidal mixing front is a transition between stratified and vertically mixed water created by variations in tidal mixing. On one side of the front, the tidal currents are not strong enough to mix the sun's heat down to the sea bed and the water becomes stratified, with a warm layer lying on top of a colder layer. On the other side of the front, the tides are strong enough to mix the sun's heat to the sea bed and the water is vertically mixed. At the front, there is a strong gradient of sea surface temperature and other water properties.

Tidal range is the vertical distance between low and high tide.

Turbulence is a random motion of water superimposed on the mean flow of the tide. Turbulence can be thought of as a series of eddies, or whirlpools, added to the mean flow. The eddies transfer parcels of water from one part of the flow to another. Material dissolved in the water is also transferred and so the turbulence mixes the sea, smoothing out gradients.

About the author:

David Bowers grew up in North Wales and now lives close to the sea in Pembrokeshire. He is Emeritus Professor of Physical Oceanography at Bangor University, where he taught courses on tides and oceanography for over 30 years. He is the co-author of two other books: *Introducing Oceanography* (with David Thomas, published by Dunedin Academic Press) and *Tides: A Very Short Introduction* (with Emyr Martyn Roberts, published by Oxford University Press). He was scientific advisor to a recent television series about the tide (Llanw, produced by Cwmni Da in Caernarfon and shown internationally) and has written a popular account of the tides of the North Wales coast in the magazine *Maritime Wales*.

Jean Napier

Bardsey

Now and Then

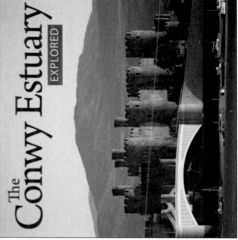

The

Conwy Estuary

EXPLORED

COMPACT CYMRU

COMPACT CYMRU

– MORE TITLES:

www.carreg-gwalch.cymru

Llŷn
the peninsula and its past EXPLORED

Pembrokeshire
its present and its past EXPLORED

Geraint Jenkins

Smugglers in Wales

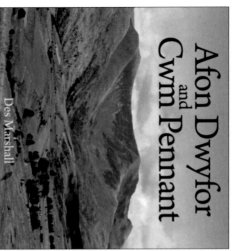

Afon Dwyfor
and
Cwm Pennant

Des Marshall

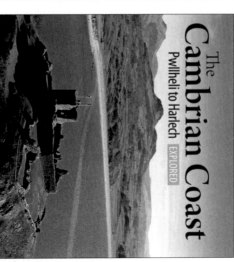

The
Cambrian Coast
Pwllheli to Harlech EXPLORED

Snowdonia's
Waterfalls

Des Marshall

Old Bridges
of Snowdonia

Des Marshall